It Happened to Me

Series Editor: Arlene Hirschfelder

Books in the It Happened to Me series are designed for inquisitive teens digging for answers about certain illnesses, social issues, or lifestyle interests. Whether you are deep into your teen years or just entering them, these books are gold mines of up-to-date information, riveting teen views, and great visuals to help you figure out stuff. Besides special boxes highlighting singular facts, each book is enhanced with the latest reading lists, Web sites, and an index. Perfect for browsing, these books contain loads of expert information by acclaimed writers to help parents, guardians, and librarians understand teen illness, tough situations, and lifestyle choices.

1. *Epilepsy: The Ultimate Teen Guide,* by Kathlyn Gay and Sean McGarrahan, 2002.
2. *Stress Relief: The Ultimate Teen Guide,* by Mark Powell, 2002.
3. *Learning Disabilities: The Ultimate Teen Guide,* by Penny Hutchins Paquette and Cheryl Gerson Tuttle, 2003.
4. *Making Sexual Decisions: The Ultimate Teen Guide,* by L. Kris Gowen, 2003.
5. *Asthma: The Ultimate Teen Guide,* by Penny Hutchins Paquette, 2003.
6. *Cultural Diversity—Conflicts and Challenges: The Ultimate Teen Guide,* by Kathlyn Gay, 2003.
7. *Diabetes: The Ultimate Teen Guide,* by Katherine J. Moran, 2004.
8. *When Will I Stop Hurting? Teens, Loss, and Grief: The Ultimate Teen Guide to Dealing with Grief,* by Ed Myers, 2004.
9. *Volunteering: The Ultimate Teen Guide,* by Kathlyn Gay, 2004.
10. *Organ Transplants—A Survival Guide for the Entire Family: The Ultimate Teen Guide,* by Tina P. Schwartz, 2005.

Obsessive-Compulsive Disorder

The Ultimate Teen Guide

NATALIE ROMPELLA

It Happened to Me, No. 25

The Scarecrow Press, Inc.
Lanham, Maryland • Toronto • Plymouth, UK
2009

SCARECROW PRESS, INC.

Published in the United States of America
by Scarecrow Press, Inc.
A wholly owned subsidiary of
The Rowman & Littlefield Publishing Group, Inc.
4501 Forbes Boulevard, Suite 200, Lanham, Maryland 20706
www.scarecrowpress.com

Estover Road
Plymouth PL6 7PY
United Kingdom

British Library Cataloguing in Publication Information Available

Library of Congress Cataloging-in-Publication Data

Rompella, Natalie.
  Obsessive-compulsive disorder : the ultimate teen guide / Natalie Rompella.
    p. cm. — (It happened to me ; no. 25)
  Includes bibliographical references and index.
  ISBN-13: 978-0-8108-5778-0 (cloth : alk. paper)
  ISBN-10: 0-8108-5778-2 (cloth : alk. paper)
  ISBN-13: 978-0-8108-6720-8 (ebook)
  ISBN-10: 0-8108-6720-6 (ebook)
  1. Obsessive-compulsive disorder—Popular works. I. Title.
  RC553.R66 2009
  616.85'227—dc22   2008046242

∞™ The paper used in this publication meets the minimum requirements of
American National Standard for Information Sciences—Permanence of Paper
for Printed Library Materials, ANSI/NISO Z39.48–1992.
Manufactured in the United States of America.

Contents

Contents

Foreword

WHY I WROTE THIS BOOK

We all have quirks about us. You can't let your broccoli touch your mashed potatoes. You don't step on sidewalk cracks. One of mine is that after I lock my car doors and walk away, I walk right back to make sure I really did lock the car. Does this impact my life? Not horribly.

While taking a psychology class in college, I read Judith Rapoport's *The Boy Who Couldn't Stop Washing*. The book shares different people's struggles with obsessive-compulsive disorder (OCD). The fact that I used to call my mom from school to make sure my curling iron was turned off was child's play compared with what the people in the book went through. Some people were convinced that they had run someone over with their car and needed to retrace their path. One woman spent her school years filling in all the spaces in the middles of letters (such as *o, p,* and *d*) and had the compulsion to count to fifty between each word she read. Can you imagine if this were your life? What if you had no idea it was OCD and that it could be treated?

As an educator, I have a soft spot for children and teens. They are trying so hard to make sense of the world, and the last thing they need is something weighing them down the way OCD can.

What's great about books is that they offer advice and knowledge without anyone else needing to know you are looking for it. If you have a question, you can usually find the answer in a book. Yes, the Internet is also great for that, but anything can be posted there, and some postings speak less accurately or truthfully than a book with credible sources. Books can be shared with others or kept hidden under your bed.

As I found out while trying to locate teens to write passages for my book, many people who have OCD still don't want to share their secret. In looking for teens to write anonymously, I posted my request on many different Listservs, in newsletters, and at support groups, but I received very few responses. If that many teens who know they have OCD are less than willing to want to share their struggles, imagine how hard it is for teens who haven't even started to seek help yet. My hope is that they come across my book. I hope they can see that they are not alone. They shouldn't feel embarrassed or feel that they are horrible people because of their thoughts or actions. Maybe it can help them seek professional help or tell a parent what they go through on a daily basis. If even one teen does this, my book is a success.

HOW TO USE THIS BOOK

This book is not meant to replace seeing a trained mental health professional with expertise in OCD. It is to help you understand what OCD is, how common it is, what types of treatment are available, and how to get help. *You should not attempt to treat yourself.*

In some of the chapters, you will read firsthand accounts by teens and adults with OCD. Some accounts were given by teens soon after they learned they had OCD; others are by teens or adults sharing their paths to improvement. Their names have been changed to protect their privacy.

MY PERSONAL EXPERIENCE

I wasn't diagnosed with OCD until I was an adult. One reason for this is that when I was a child, it wasn't as commonly recognized and diagnosed as it is today. In addition, I was able to live without major interruptions in my life. My main treatment was in the form of medication, mainly for anxiety, but I've worked hard on overcoming my obsessions and compulsions using cognitive behavioral therapy (CBT), which we will talk about in chapter 9.

It wasn't until I attended the Obsessive-Compulsive Foundation's (OCF's) annual national conference that I realized how much I still suffered from OCD. I will talk about the conference again in chapter 13; attending the conference is a great way to receive information, as well as to meet others with OCD who are at different stages of treatment.

As I looked around at the other attendees, I found it interesting how many lives were affected by the disorder. No one stood out as mentally ill; any one of the people who attended looked like someone I'd see at the movie theater or the grocery store. Although I attended the conference as part of my research for this book, I was surprised to discover how much I still had to learn about myself. I decided to start a list of all the different experiences I've had:

- As a child, I said the Our Father and the Hail Mary, as well as a personal prayer for deceased relatives. If I made a mistake or didn't say one of the prayers perfectly, such as stalling when blessing one of my relatives, I'd have to start over, or I feared that someone else would die. This happened nightly.

- If I touched an object, such as a light switch, I had to be sure that it symmetrically touched my hand, not with more pressure on one side of my hand than on the other. If it did, I'd touch it again to get it right.

- I had to walk down the stairs "properly"—and in my case that meant I was compelled to skip over the creaky step and slide my hand down the railing with the correct amount of pressure.

- I had (and still have) a fear of contamination. In public restrooms, I'm quite talented at flushing the toilet with my foot, regardless of whether it is a button 5 feet off the ground; I can open just about any door with my pinky finger (I figure if any finger can risk getting dirty, it's the one I don't eat with); and at someone else's house, I use the part of the hand towel that other people don't use (the back half on the inside of the towel). I also wash my hands often, keep my nails short, avoid touching objects with my fingertips, and throw out objects if they seem dirty. My students once caught me washing off my stapler with soap and water after it had fallen in the wastebasket (at least I didn't decide to leave it there!).

⊚ Here's the one that uses up the most of my time: I am a checker. The items I most often check are that the water is turned off, the toilet is not running, my pet guinea pigs have food and water and I have put them back in their cage after they have played, the iron is off, the stove is off, the doors are locked, my garage door is shut, the refrigerator is completely closed, my car doors are locked, and I remembered to bring my cell phone with me. I don't need to check all of these before I do something; it often depends on my stress level or what I am doing. Leaving for a vacation is the worst. Once, when I lived in an apartment complex, I was doing my usual checking routine of rattling my doorknob to be sure I locked up and heard one of my neighbors yell from his apartment, "It's locked!" Yikes!

⊚ As a child, I was sometimes afraid I would sleepwalk and stab my parents. (Believe it or not, this is a form of OCD that deals with unwanted thoughts.)

⊚ I sometimes straighten things up; I don't like certain things left in disarray. Corners of small objects need to be parallel with the object they are sitting on. Surprisingly, this is only true of particular objects—I am in no way a neat freak (or even neat, for that matter!).

⊚ I hoard objects: books, clothes, papers, college binders, and textbooks. What if I need that notebook from college about Olduvai Gorge someday?

It's shocking when you write down a list like this. I hope that by pouring my heart out like this, maybe you learn a little bit more about the different forms OCD can take—and that things can get better.

Acknowledgments

I would like to thank the teens who wrote passages for my book. It took a lot of courage for them to share their personal stories with the world. By doing this, they may have helped someone else conquer his or her own personal struggle with OCD. And for that, they are heroes.

I would also like to thank Dr. Karen Cassiday for reading my manuscript for accuracy. I knew that with her impressive experience with anxiety disorders as a clinical psychologist, she could really help me make this book an accurate source of information for teens. In addition, I'd like to give a shout out to Phoebe Moore, PhD, a clinical psychologist who specializes in treating OCD in children and adolescents. She also worked on the Pediatric OCD Treatment Study II (POTS II), and read my manuscript for accuracy.

Another thanks goes to psychotherapist Melanie Justice, who also happens to be my sister. She answered various questions I had, and also wrote a passage in chapter 8.

Merci to J. David Jentsch, PhD, associate professor of psychology and psychiatry & biobehavioral sciences at UCLA (University of California, Los Angeles), who read chapter 4 for accuracy.

And, last, two "thank yous" go out to my editors: my mom, Joann Rompella, and my editor at Scarecrow Press, Arlene Hirschfelder, who both not only could find an error in a grammar book but helped cheer me on (and who will both probably find something grammatically incorrect with this sentence).

This book would not have been possible without the help of those mentioned above to answer my questions and supply technical information.

1 Obsessive-Compulsive Disorder

MARY

Mary comes late to first-period English every day. She always has a different excuse for why she isn't there before the bell rings. If you were to look at her hands you might know why she's always late: Unlike her tanned face and legs, her hands are red, raw, and chapped.

Mary seems to have it all together. She's on the cheerleading squad, gets straight As, and made homecoming court. What her classmates don't know is how out of control she feels.

Mary suffers from an obsession with germs and contamination and a compulsion to wash her hands repeatedly. She feels anxiety any time she touches a doorknob, picks something up off the floor, or grazes the surface of her desk with even her fingertips. She can picture all the germs crawling around the school and onto her hands. She knows those desks haven't been cleaned in ages. She even puts a piece of notebook paper down before setting her books on the desk to "protect" them from contamination.

She uses waterless sanitizer throughout the day and washes her hands in the bathroom between every class. When she gets home, she scrubs her hands and arms up to her elbows over and over with an antibacterial soap. If she had a really bad experience with germs that day, she even rubs a little bleach on a washcloth and wipes it over her hands.

Mary doesn't want to be this way. She wishes she could be as carefree as other people in her class. She watches with envy as her friend Julia pours a package of M&Ms on her desk and eats

1

them. As much as she wants to be like Julia—and even to wash her hands only once instead of repeatedly—her mind talks her into washing over and over again.

Mary has kept this a secret from her friends since she was a child. Although she often had the compulsion to perform actions in sets of five, her issues with contamination were triggered freshman year when she watched a video in health class about the importance of germ prevention. She went home that day and showered for forty minutes. Now her problem has spiraled out of control. Some of her closest friends sometimes catch her doing "strange" things, such as pressing elevator buttons with her knuckle or insisting on stopping at her house to use the bathroom before going out after basketball games, but Mary doesn't want to tell anyone about her problem.

Her parents wish they could do something to help her. Her mom has taken to washing Mary's clothes separately from the rest of the family's due to Mary's insistence that her brother's and her parents' clothes were contaminated. In fact, Mary won't even touch her dirty clothes after she has taken them off, leaving them in a pile on her closet floor. Her mother knows that she probably isn't helping by picking them up and putting them in the laundry room, but she doesn't know what else to do.

DO YOU HAVE OCD?

Mary is fictional, but she represents people everywhere who suffer from OCD. This disorder affects many children, teens, and adults all over the world. It compels people to wash, check to see if appliances are turned off, and count objects and steps taken over and over again. Sometimes it causes people to hoard items until the piles fill rooms.

The disorder usually involves both obsessions and compulsions. Obsessions are ideas, thoughts, or emotions that are usually unwanted and uncontrollable. They often create anxiety and discomfort. Some people are obsessed with thoughts of germs; others worry that they have left the water running. Some obsess that they have caused or may cause harm, have molested or may molest another person, or are secretly homosexual.

Compulsions are actions that are sometimes uncontrollable and usually unwanted. For example, people who have obsessions about germs often have compulsions to repeatedly wash their hands, clothing, and floors. Objects that were used in public, such as credit cards, money, and pens, are also troublesome for such people. They can be thought of as contaminated because others have touched them, they have fallen on the ground, or they are not cleaned often. People who have obsessions about leaving the water running often repeatedly check to see whether they did leave it running. Washing your hands once or checking once that the water is turned off is not unusual for most people. However, people with a compulsion may wash their hands one hundred times a day or continue to drive back to their house to check over and over to make sure they really did turn the water off.

Not all compulsions are actions. Some people have mental compulsions, such as counting or praying in their head. These are called mental rituals.

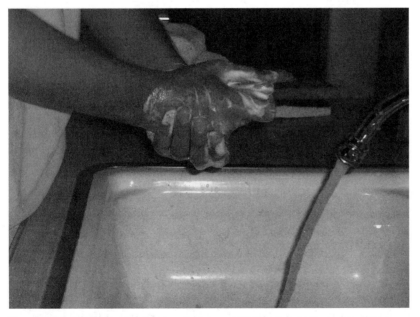

People who obsess about germs may wash their hands over and over again. Photo by Natalie Rompella.

3

Most people have thoughts and actions that they might refer to as obsessive and/or compulsive.

Right now you might not be able to tell the difference between a normal thought and an OCD thought. Are you washing your hands because they are really dirty or because your OCD is telling you to do it? OCD can disguise itself so it seems like normal thoughts. Here's a comparison. Imagine you see an e-mail addressed to you from someone you've never heard of before. Once you open it, you realize it's spam. The next time it sees an e-mail from the same name, the non-OCD brain knows to simply delete it. On the other hand, in our comparison, the OCD brain can't tell the difference between "friendly" messages and "spam" messages similar to ones already received. The OCD brain opens all "messages," even the ones that are false messages telling you to do unneeded actions.

OCD is diagnosed as a problem when it takes up an hour or more a day, it causes difficulty with daily activities, and the actions that are being performed are not for pleasure.

OCD can cause people to avoid situations in which they are afraid their OCD will be triggered. It can slow down tasks they are trying to complete if they are perseverating (repeating uncontrollably) on a thought or are completing an unwanted action. They can be late to get places because of rituals they are performing. The ways it can affect a person's life are nearly endless.

DID YOU KNOW?

Have you ever heard of the famous evolutionist Charles Darwin? He is thought to have had OCD. And what about Florence Nightingale, the nurse who helped to raise sanitation concerns?[1] In her case, maybe it was her OCD that helped push those sanitation standards forward.

Wrigley Field, the home of the Chicago Cubs, holds more than forty thousand people. The number of Americans with OCD would fill the stadium seats more than eighty-two times. Photo courtesy of John Bosch.

YOU ARE NOT ALONE

Believe it or not, OCD affects between 1 and 5 percent of American teens.[2] That means you're probably not the only one at your school or job to have it. There is even a chance that someone you know has OCD and is trying to deal with it just as you are. *More people have OCD than have diabetes or asthma.*[3] Why, then, don't we know many people who have the disorder? Unfortunately, some people are ashamed or don't even know why they perform certain actions, and so they keep their condition a secret. Others are not correctly diagnosed with having OCD and think they don't have it.

Out of every forty people, one has OCD. It can affect any of us, regardless of where we live, how rich or poor we are, or how old we are. However, most cases of OCD begin before age thirty. These trends are the same in other cultures. [4]

OCD is not something to be ashamed of. Doctors now know what to look for to diagnose OCD, and there are effective ways of treating it. Knowing what you can do to control it can make a world of difference in how you live your life. *It is estimated that the success rate for patients willing to fully engage themselves in treatment (exposure with response prevention or*

ERP) *is 75 to 80 percent.*[5] (We'll talk more about exposure with response prevention in chapter 9.)

OCD has been around for a long time. So why are there still so many people out there who are undiagnosed? As mentioned before, people are often embarrassed about their obsessions and compulsions and don't want to share what they are going through with others, not even with professionals. Some people still have never heard of OCD. But thanks to exposure through the media, OCD is becoming more well-known. In the foreword to *Everything in Its Place*, the

THE HISTORY OF OCD

Even as far back as the ninth century, OCD must have been prevalent enough to have its own special name. It was then that a Persian physician named Unhammad came up with nine categories of mental illness, including "febrile delirium" (similar to what is known as schizophrenia),[6] "manic restlessness," "persecutory psychosis" (paranoia), "lovesickness with anxiety and depression," and "disorders of judgment." Included in these was a category called *murrae souda*, which included worrying and needing to repeat certain behaviors, similar to what we call OCD today.[7]

YOU GOTTA READ THIS!

Imagine having a fear of contamination while hosting a show that involves kids getting covered in green goo, baked beans, and raw eggs. It's not every day that a celebrity is willing to share with the world a secret about him- or herself that is so personal that it could impact his or her career. Marc Summers does just that in his autobiography, *Everything in Its Place: My Trials and Triumphs with Obsessive Compulsive Disorder*. A lifelong sufferer of OCD, Summers, the host for years of *Double Dare*, a kids' show on Nickelodeon, didn't know there was a name for what he went through until he met a doctor who specialized in OCD who was about to be a guest on Summers's talk show. This book is a great read, both to learn what it was like for Summers to have OCD and be in the public eye and also to get facts on the disorder.

Marc Summers, the host of _Double Dare_ on Nickelodeon. Photo courtesy of MTV Networks.

autobiography of TV personality Marc Summers, Eric Hollander, MD, notes that 25 percent of people with OCD actually end up seeking treatment after hearing about it in the news, in a magazine, on television, or in other media.[8]

Speaking of celebrities—did you realize that there are many famous people who have OCD and are still affected by it? Radio talk show host Howard Stern used to have issues with ritualistic behavior such as reading sentences three times and performing actions by using the right (not left) side of his body. He also has an obsession about germs.[9] You might have heard of Howard Hughes; the movie _The Aviator_ was about his life. He was a famous businessman. His obsessions and compulsions

> ### YOU GOTTA READ THIS!
>
> ### *Washing My Life Away: Surviving Obsessive-Compulsive Disorder*, by Ruth Deane
>
> **How would you feel if no one you knew had ever heard of OCD? This is what happened to Ruth. She grew up in England and lived a happy, normal childhood, full of muddy and dirty moments. Then one day, at eighteen, she became overwhelmed with worries that required her to check household appliances. She began having fears of contamination. Her fears became so severe that she was hardly able to eat food, even if she prepared it herself. Her rituals occupied most of her day. Her saving grace was seeking medical attention, where, over time, she finally returned to a functional lifestyle.**

got so out of hand that he spent years of his life holed up in his penthouse with his house crew helping take care of his compulsions. (If only he had known about behavior therapy, discussed in chapter 9). Other stars with OCD include Roseanne Barr and Howie Mandel.

HELP IS AVAILABLE

There are many different forms of treatment for OCD. The first step is recognizing that you need help. The second step is admitting that you cannot do it alone. If you've kept your OCD a secret, it is time to share your situation with someone you trust, such as a parent or medical professional.

Your doctor will recommend a course of treatment appropriate for you based on your personal situation. The different types of treatment available are discussed in detail in chapters 9–11. Medication is often not a doctor's first choice for treatment. Although treatments other than medication—such as exposure with response prevention therapy—may seem like a lot of work, you may find that they are able to help you relieve many of your symptoms without taking medication.

8

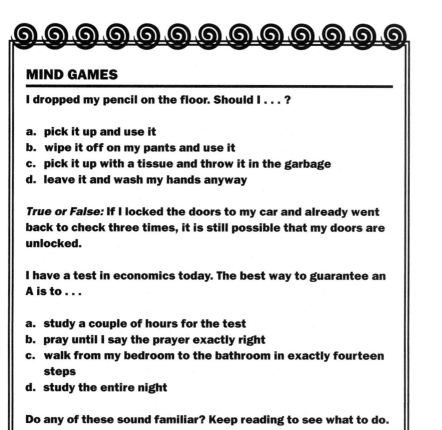

MIND GAMES

I dropped my pencil on the floor. Should I . . . ?

a. pick it up and use it
b. wipe it off on my pants and use it
c. pick it up with a tissue and throw it in the garbage
d. leave it and wash my hands anyway

True or False: If I locked the doors to my car and already went back to check three times, it is still possible that my doors are unlocked.

I have a test in economics today. The best way to guarantee an A is to . . .

a. study a couple of hours for the test
b. pray until I say the prayer exactly right
c. walk from my bedroom to the bathroom in exactly fourteen steps
d. study the entire night

Do any of these sound familiar? Keep reading to see what to do.

QUESTIONS AND ANSWERS

If you are just learning about OCD, you probably have lots of questions. Here are some common questions people often ask about OCD:

Q: *What does OCD stand for?*
A: Obsessive-compulsive disorder, an anxiety disorder.

Q: *How do I know if I have OCD?*
A: Many people have tendencies to check things more than they need to or to wash their hands many times in a day. This does not mean that they have OCD. A true diagnosis can be made only by a professional. The rule of thumb in making a diagnosis is that your obsessions (fearing germs, fearing a certain number,

etc.) and/or compulsions (such as washing, checking, or praying) take up more than one hour a day. (The book used by mental health professionals with a list of symptoms for mental health disorders is the *Diagnostic and Statistical Manual of Mental Disorders* [DSM-IV-TR]). If you feel that your condition is causing too much distress or is making work or school difficult, it wouldn't hurt to talk to somebody about it.

Q: *How do I know it's OCD and not something else—like schizophrenia?*
A: It is hard for you to make a diagnosis on yourself, and only a professional can give you an accurate diagnosis. The basic difference, however, between OCD and disorders like schizophrenia is that people with OCD know that the actions they are performing and the thoughts they are having are irrational and cause anxiety, whereas people with schizophrenia and other psychotic disorders do not find their thoughts irrational. If your condition is impacting your life, you probably want to seek help from a mental health professional. This is explained in more detail in chapter 8.

Q: *How many people have OCD?*
A: More than 5 million people (both diagnosed and undiagnosed) in the United States alone experience symptoms of OCD.[10]

Q: *Isn't it good to wash my hands often or check to make sure I turned off the lights?*
A: It is good to do those things. The problem with OCD is that people who have it feel compelled to do these things over and over, which takes up a large chunk of their life and causes a lot of distress.

Q: *How did I get it?*
A: OCD may be hereditary and it is biological. This means it was not caused by your mom always reminding you to wash your hands. It happens when parts of the brain are more active than they need to be and do not "screen out" false messages the

way they should. There is also a type of OCD that can be triggered by a strep infection, called PANDAS (pediatric autoimmune neuropsychiatric disorders associated with streptococcal infections). See chapters 3 and 4 to learn more.

Q: *Can my OCD be cured?*
A: Unfortunately, no. But you can learn strategies to help you break the cycle of your obsessions and compulsions.

Q: *Is OCD hereditary?*
A: Scientists do believe that parents with OCD are more likely to have children with OCD than are parents who don't have it. The specific type of OCD (such as a fear of washing or a compulsion to make things symmetrical) does not seem to be hereditary, however: A parent who has fears of contamination might have a child who feels compelled to check that appliances are turned off. And not all parents with OCD will have children with OCD.

Q: *Is OCD contagious?*
A: No. You can't "catch" OCD from someone else.

Q: *My obsession is very embarrassing, and my family would be mad if they knew what it was. What should I do?*
A: OCD seems to pick an obsession that it knows will get to you. People who love their family may have thoughts of harming or doing something inappropriate to members of their family. It does not make you a bad person or mean you really believe these things deep down. It is a good idea to tell your therapist about these thoughts so he or she can help you learn how to manage them.

Q: *I keep having horrible sexual thoughts about family members. Does that really mean I'm attracted to them?*
A: Absolutely not! OCD works in strange ways and often bugs you with thoughts you would never have without OCD. Read more about this type of OCD in chapter 2, in the section titled "Other Forms of OCD."

WHAT IS A MENTAL ILLNESS?

When you hear the phrase "mental illness," it might make you think of insane asylums, people hallucinating, or the book or movie *Girl, Interrupted*. Mental illness is a disorder involving the mind rather than the body (which is called physical illness). When you are physically ill—such as when you have a cold, your asthma's acting up, or you have an ingrown toenail—you go to a person trained in helping heal the body, often a doctor. The same is true for people with mental illnesses: They often see a specialist as well—a psychologist, a psychiatrist, or a therapist. Examples of other mental illnesses are attention-deficit/hyperactivity disorder (ADHD), depression, schizophrenia, autism, anorexia nervosa, and post-traumatic stress disorder. Each mental illness has a unique set of criteria. To be accurately diagnosed, you will need to see a mental health professional.

Since OCD involves the mind, it is considered a mental illness. This does not mean you are crazy or that you should be institutionalized (although as you read on, you'll find that institutionalization was often a solution in the past, before mental illnesses were better understood). Often, however, it does mean that you will need help from a mental health professional to conquer the illness.

Until recently, doctors considered OCD a neurotic condition. The term "neurotic" is somewhat generic. It includes people with mental disabilities who are able to function in society, as opposed to those diagnosed as psychotic, who are most likely unable to function in society. It's been only about twenty years since OCD was finally understood to be a unique anxiety disorder.

Q: *If I have OCD, do I have to go to a mental hospital?*
A: It depends on the severity of your OCD. There are people who cannot function and need the help offered in a full-time facility. There are special hospitals for patients with OCD—they are not the scary insane asylums shown in horror movies. However, the majority of people with OCD are able to work on resisting their obsessions and compulsions while living their regular lifestyle.

Q: *If I have OCD, should I see a therapist?*
A: Many people with OCD find seeing a therapist helpful. A therapist can first diagnose you with OCD and then develop a plan for you to help manage your compulsions.

Q: *Will I need to take medication?*
A: Not everyone who has OCD needs to take medication to experience improvement in his or her symptoms. A therapy called ERP is often recommended instead of medication. Some people take medicines to help with other disorders that commonly occur with OCD, such as depression or other anxiety disorders, so they can work on treating their OCD. (Sometimes these other disorders can cause people to have trouble completing their ERP. Combining ERP with medication helps them to feel better so they can work on their ERP more effectively.) See chapter 10 for more information about medication.

Q: *Can I still go to college?*
A: Chances are, yes—unless you have such a severe case that you have difficulty functioning in a school setting, you should be able to go to college. You may need some modifications and therapy, but that shouldn't stop you from reaching your dreams. See chapter 6 for more information about school.

Q: *Should I tell my teachers/professors about my condition?*
A: It depends. If it isn't impacting you at school, you may not want to. If it is, you may want to start by talking to a school or disability counselor. See chapter 6 for more discussion about this.

Q: *How come I act on my OCD only at home and not at school?*
A: Everyone is different. You might be able to control your OCD in front of friends but find that you must release the buildup of anxiety as soon as you walk in your front door. OCD symptoms also become more prevalent when you are stressed, tired, or anxious.

Q: *Should I tell my friends?*
A: Some people with OCD feel comfortable sharing this with close friends; others don't. You will have to decide whether you want to tell them and if you think they will be understanding.

Q: *How long has OCD been around?*
A: A long time! The name obsessive-compulsive disorder is more recent, but there is evidence dating back to the ninth century that people had similar symptoms to OCD. It wasn't until the 1950s that OCD was recognized in *DSM* as a type of anxiety disorder. Treatments have also advanced through the years. The most common nowadays is ERP therapy.

Q: *Is OCD what Jack Nicholson has in the movie* As Good as It Gets?
A: He has some symptoms of OCD, although he also may be thought of as having obsessive-compulsive personality disorder (OCPD). See chapter 12 for details.

ELIZABETH MCINGVALE: MAKING A DIFFERENCE

In 2006 the Obsessive-Compulsive Foundation (OCF) began a new campaign. Its purpose: to show people, especially teens, that OCD can affect anyone, regardless of age, race, or background. Elizabeth McIngvale became the national spokesperson for the OCF's new public awareness campaign.

Elizabeth was thirteen when she was first diagnosed with OCD. She suffered mainly from obsessions related to fear of contamination and to the numbers forty-two and six. She felt compelled to wash her hands one hundred times a day, as well as perform actions in sets of forty-two, such as washing her hands or locking a door forty-two times. Because this was impacting her life so greatly, she chose to get help at the Menninger Clinic in Houston, Texas.

When asked, "Why the number forty-two?" she responds:

At the particular time that I was struggling tremendously with numbers, my mother was forty-two. I actually had a lot of trouble with the number six. So anything that was related to

What Does OCD Look Like?

Me.
My Name is
Elizabeth.

WWW.
OCD
GET
HELP
.org

Seven million children and adults
in the United States suffer from
Obsessive Compulsive Disorder.

DON'T SUFFER IN SILENCE.

**Elizabeth McIngvale, the national spokesperson for the OCF.
Photo courtesy of the OCF.**

the number six was a really bad number for me. That would
have included the number forty-two because four plus two is
six. However every number up to forty-two I couldn't seem to
stop at. I always found an issue there. But when I came to forty-
two I had to stop there, because I simply justified that since it
was my mom's age it would be okay to not go any further.

Since her treatment at Menniger, Elizabeth has been able to
prevent OCD from taking over her life and is helping others to
do the same. She has appeared on local television news

A PERSONAL STORY
Elizabeth, age twenty

Being the national spokesperson for the Obsessive-Compulsive Foundation has not only been an amazing experience, but a time to learn, to help, and to grow. I have had the opportunity to do great things that I would have never imagined, like appearing on various TV shows and appearing on a national ad campaign both in print and TV. I have been able to speak on various radio shows and have appeared on local shows and newspapers and various Internet and magazine articles. But none of this is what matters—in fact, I wouldn't have done any of it without the end result in mind: being able to help others. Through this experience I have learned that life can be tough, it can be really tough, but there's a reason for everything. Good can always come out of a bad situation, even when it seems nearly impossible. I would have never imagined good out of my personal struggle with OCD. But when I open my inbox and see e-mails from kids, teenagers and adults that I have inspired, I know I am doing the right thing.

If I can give any advice, however, the most important thing to do, in my opinion, is to get to know someone else who has OCD. When I was diagnosed at age thirteen, I was lost and felt alone. I didn't know anyone else who had OCD and had never even met anyone else [who had it]. My mom ran across a Sports Illustrated *article that forever changed my life. It was an article about a college basketball player, Julian, who struggled with OCD as well. As my mom read the article, she felt like she was reading about me. Matching rituals and descriptions that we both shared made my mom realize I had to meet him. I did, and that single moment changed everything for me. I was able to have someone I looked up to who struggled like I did and who understood what I was going through. He explained that everything would be okay and there was help out there.*

I later checked into the Menninger clinic and continued outpatient therapy [with a doctor from Menninger]. Two inpatient hospital visits later and intensive outpatient treatment, I still remember the day I met Julian like it was yesterday. For after that I finally knew that I could do it. I could wake up every day and say I'm not alone and although I have to fight my OCD today and tomorrow, I know I have the strength to do so. He also showed me what I wanted to do. If I could ever be the person for someone else that he was to me, then this is my calling. This is what I am meant to do and he showed me that.

Julian is now my boyfriend and someone who I admire dearly. He is the one who taught me the most important thing in this battle: It's okay. It's okay to have OCD; it's something not to be ashamed of! E-mail me, call me—whatever you do, don't suffer alone. You don't have to!![11]

programs and in newspapers in her hometown of Houston, as well as in magazines such as *Sweet 16* and on satellite radio. She also has appeared on TV for a public service announcement on OCD and on various talk shows, including *Dr. Phil*, *Good Morning America*, *The View*, *Inside Edition*, and *Paula Zahn Now*. Besides her role as the OCF's national spokesperson, she also is the founder and president of her own nonprofit organization, the Peace of Mind Foundation.

"I want to be able to do for others what doctors have done for me—save their lives."—Elizabeth McIngvale, age twenty

But what is Elizabeth most proud of? "I am most proud of the support group that I run bimonthly in Houston, Texas. I dedicate my time to helping and serving others who have a mental illness and who struggle just like I do. It's okay to have OCD, and it's okay to have something that needs work. But it's not okay to feel alone, because you don't have to!"

Twenty-one years old in 2008, Elizabeth is a student at Loyola University Chicago, majoring in social work. She hopes to also attain her master's in social work and continue on to become a specialist in OCD. (To contact Elizabeth, go to her Web site: www.peaceofmind.com).

NOTES

1. OCD-UK, "What Is Obsessive-Compulsive Disorder?" www.ocduk.org/1/ocd.htm (accessed July 27, 2007).

2. Mitzi Waltz, *Obsessive-Compulsive Disorder: Help for Children and Adolescents* (Sebastopol, CA: O'Reilly & Associates, 2000), 2.

3. Jeffrey M. Schwartz, *Brain Lock: Free Yourself from Obsessive-Compulsive Disorder* (New York: ReganBooks, 1996), xiv.

4. Bruce M. Hyman and Cherry Pedrich, *Obsessive-Compulsive Disorder* (Brookfield, CT: Twenty-First Century Books, 2003), 19–20.

5. Ellen Thackery and Madeline Harris, eds., *Gale Encyclopedia of Mental Disorders* (Detroit, MI: Thomson Gale, 2003), 689–90.

6. S. R. Parkar, V. S. Dawani, and J. S. Apte, "History of Psychiatry in India," *Journal of Postgraduate Medicine* 47, no. 1 (2001): 73. Available online at www.jpgmonline.com/text.asp?2001/47/1/73/226 (accessed July 2, 2008).

7. Michael H. Stone, *Healing the Mind: A History of Psychiatry from Antiquity to the Present* (New York: W. W. Norton, 1997), 18.

8. Marc Summers, *Everything in Its Place: My Trials and Triumphs with Obsessive Compulsive Disorder* (New York: Jeremy P. Tarcher/Putnam, 1999), xv.

9. Howard Stern, *Miss America* (New York: ReganBooks, 1995), 104, 110–11.

10. OCF, "Questions & Answers about Obsessive Compulsive Disorders," www.ocfoundation.org/UserFiles/File/Questions-Answers-About-OCD.pdf (accessed July 25, 2008).

11. Throughout this book, you will find passages written by teens—and, in one case, an adult—reflecting on their experiences with OCD. These letters are printed in italics. The names of the writers have been changed, except for the OCF national spokesperson Elizabeth McIngvale. You will notice that the teens are at various stages of treatment—some are just beginning; others have been through CBT (discussed further in chapter 9).

Types of OCD

A PERSONAL STORY
Michelle, age sixteen

I was diagnosed with obsessive-compulsive disorder exactly two years ago. It wasn't until then, the summer going into my freshman year of high school, that my OCD was triggered to a crisis level, and was therefore detected for the first time. I suffered mainly from obsessions and compulsions surrounding germs, getting "contaminated," and perfectionism. I would worry that I would contaminate myself and everything around me if I had touched things or been around things I considered dirty (trashcans, faucets, doorknobs, cigarette smoke, urine, feces . . .). I knew that my thoughts were irrational, yet I still obsessed about the things that bothered me and carried out compulsions by avoiding touching certain objects and endlessly washing my hands and showering for extremely long amounts of time.

My fears around perfectionism surrounded [worries of] plagiarizing, taking the easy way out of assignments for school, and saying something that was either mean or did not accurately represent something that either happened or was said. It took me hours and hours to complete school assignments, as I read and reread everything, and spent hours checking and rechecking my work. I constantly sought reassurance about my contamination and perfectionism concerns from others, and still tried to reassure myself through the use of mental rituals. Getting through the day was very difficult, as every moment of the day I was preoccupied by the OCD in some way.

Over the years many different forms of OCD have been discovered and diagnosed. The most common forms are checking; cleaning; counting, touching, or repeating; and hoarding. Other forms include praying, arranging, and having unwanted thoughts.

People with OCD often feel alone and helpless. Photo courtesy of istockphoto.com/ Mikael Damkier.

"Most people with OCD have several types of obsessions, or even most types. This is normal for OCD. It does not mean that your OCD is harder to treat, just that you'll have more targets to aim to treat."
—Karen Cassiday, PhD, clinical psychologist and a founding fellow in the Academy of Cognitive Therapy

CHECKING

When Eve began seventh grade, she began to have a fear that when she left her house she had not turned off her curling iron. She feared it would cause a fire that could burn down the house. She would start to worry about it during school, calling her mom on a pay phone between classes to make sure it was turned off. It always was.

Over the years, Eve's compulsions grew to include checking that the curling iron, clothes iron, faucets, and lights were turned off. She also had obsessions that she forgot to check that the house doors, car doors, garage doors, and windows were locked. She was compelled to check. It was rare that she had actually forgotten.

It became embarrassing. Eve sometimes went back to check things three or four times. She has been in public parking lots and no sooner walked away from her car before she turned back and again rattled all the car doors to make sure they were locked.

Although Eve's situation may sound extreme to someone without OCD, some people have checking rituals that take hours to complete, impacting their lives in an incapacitating way.

People who are "checkers" obsess over the thought that they forgot to perform a task, like turning off a light or locking a door. They then are compelled to check to make sure they did. Unfortunately, checking once does not satisfy them; they must check many times to be sure. Checkers fear that if they did not perform the task, something bad will happen; for example, if a house door is left unlocked, their house will be raided by burglars.

Many checkers also have fears that may seem irrational to people who don't have OCD. Some checkers fear that they have hit someone with their car. This thought is an obsession that causes them to check over and over again to see whether they actually did hit someone by driving back to where they had just been. These drivers may not only check their path but sometimes also take actions such as watching the news for reports of a hit-and-run accident.

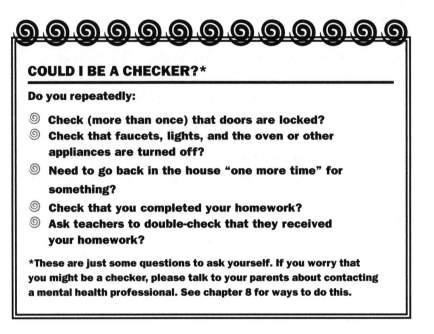

COULD I BE A CHECKER?*

Do you repeatedly:

- Check (more than once) that doors are locked?
- Check that faucets, lights, and the oven or other appliances are turned off?
- Need to go back in the house "one more time" for something?
- Check that you completed your homework?
- Ask teachers to double-check that they received your homework?

*These are just some questions to ask yourself. If you worry that you might be a checker, please talk to your parents about contacting a mental health professional. See chapter 8 for ways to do this.

Remember that although you may do some of these, it doesn't necessarily mean you have OCD. Many people check to make sure their doors are locked—as they should! The extent to which you do these actions, how much anxiety it causes when you don't, and whether it interferes with your life should help you decide whether you need to seek help.

CLEANING

Think back to the example of Mary, discussed in chapter 1, which describes a second group of people with OCD: "cleaners." These people have an obsession with germs and a compulsion to clean. This is the most common form of OCD.[1] This type of OCD occurs more often in women than in men. People with this form of OCD may not want to touch door handles, use public toilets, or shake hands with people. Although many people do not want to touch publicly used objects, people with OCD often have severe anxiety about the situation, go to extreme measures to avoid contact with objects, or stay away from public places altogether. Cleaners may shower multiple times a day or wash with harsh chemicals. They may scrub their skin raw. Cleaners may also clean objects that are touched by strangers, such as dollar bills, coins, and credit cards. They might spend hours scrubbing floors, tables, and doorknobs. They not only clean to prevent getting sick themselves, but often have fears of making others sick.

Other Forms of Contamination

A common concern often expressed by people with the cleaning variety of OCD is contamination by germs. This is not the only thing cleaners fear. More specifically, some fear the AIDS (Acquired Immune Deficiency Syndrome) virus or other specific illnesses. They may be compelled to clean after watching a movie or television program that shows someone with AIDS or another illness. Others may feel anxiety from objects (or specifically foods) that are a certain color, like red, such as ketchup.

Another contaminant to some is environmental pollution, such as radiation or asbestos. People with this form of OCD will search the house or building they are in for signs of danger. While both radiation and asbestos are dangerous, it is very unlikely that one will encounter them in normal situations.

People with this form of OCD may also have a fear that bodily secretions, such as sweat or feces, are contaminated, and avoid situations with them. (There are other forms of contamination fears; these are some of the more common ones.)

COULD I BE A CLEANER?*

Do you often:

- Take multiple showers or baths daily?
- Avoid touching writing utensils belonging to other people, door handles, or other surfaces in public?
- Avoid using public toilets?
- Avoid shaking hands?
- Wash your hands until they are chapped or red?

*These are just some questions to ask yourself. If you worry that you might be a cleaner, please talk to your parents about contacting a mental health professional. See chapter 8 for ways to do this.

Affecting Others

Sometimes keeping oneself free of contamination is enough, but people who are cleaners may also feel compelled to make sure others are "clean" as well. They may have family members strip out of the clothes they wore out in public before entering the house, have them wash their laundry separately, or be sure that they have thoroughly washed their hands before coming to the dinner table.

A study was done by scientists on "mental pollution." People were told to imagine uncomfortable situations (for example, being forced to kiss a dirty and smelly man). Afterward, some of the people felt the urge to wash.[2]

Again, many people shower multiple times a day—maybe after exercising or doing yard work—so that alone doesn't mean you are obsessed with cleaning. The reasons you are cleaning, the number of times you clean, and what you are avoiding by cleaning are facts that may help to determine whether you should be concerned.

COUNTING, TOUCHING, OR REPEATING

Have you ever had to lay a hand on an object for no apparent reason? Maybe you felt the urge to touch the object three times.

OCD BECOMES PART OF REALITY TV

Are you a fan of reality TV? In 2005 a show similar to *Big Brother* debuted in the United Kingdom. The twist: the people on the show had severe OCD. *The House of the Obsessive-Compulsives* made viewers a fly on the wall as three people worked to overcome their compulsions. One woman's OCD had kept her from being able to touch her family, including her children, because she feared contamination. You might be shocked at the treatment the therapist has each of the three people try in the house. It won't seem so strange after you've read chapter 9.

People with these forms of OCD are called "counters," and they may perform repetitive rituals because they fear being harmed or harming others if they don't, or they may just feel compelled to count objects for no particular reason—just until it "feels right" and feelings of tension subside.

Some counters feel the compulsion to count objects. Even when there are hundreds of items to count, they will. If they make an error, lose count, or think they may have made an error, they will start over. Obviously this can be quite time consuming, especially if the person is in a distracting environment.

Other counters feel the need to avoid certain types of numbers, such as odd numbers, or certain numbers, such as thirteen or a number that represents something bad that happened to them or a loved one at a certain age (maybe they lost a parent when they were fifteen years old). They then may avoid ending actions on that number. For instance, if they are doing sit-ups, they need to stop before they reach twenty. Their number could be a commonly used one, such as three. They will avoid ending on a three. They will not knock on a door three times; they may become anxious if they call someone and the person answers on three rings. This can cause problems in school: Imagine always avoiding a certain number and taking a math class. See chapter 6 for more discussion about the problems this can cause.

Another ritual people with OCD may be compelled to do is touch an object. Sometimes these "touchers" must touch the object a particular number of times; other people's compulsion is to touch the object in exactly the right way. These actions are often performed out of fear that they or someone they love might become injured or harmed if they do not. Other times, the ritual is performed just because it "feels right" to touch objects a particular way, and the person feels uncomfortable until that "right" feeling is achieved.

People with a repeating compulsion must perform actions in exactly the right way. "Repeaters" must say a prayer without errors, dot their *i*'s exactly on top, or maybe make it to the bus stop in exactly forty-five steps. If they don't, they will start all over again. Some people with this type of OCD have to complete a whole ritual before going to bed. They walk so

COULD I BE A COUNTER, TOUCHER, OR REPEATER?*

Do you often:

- Count objects for no apparent reason?
- Repeat an action a particular number of times just because you feel the urge?
- Just have to do something "one more time"?
- Need to "even up" something, never wanting to end on an odd number?
- Refuse to do certain numbered problems in school?
- Touch objects a specific number of times, beginning again if you make an error?
- Touch objects a particular way, beginning again if you make an error?
- Need to keep fixing your work until it is perfect?

*These are just some questions to ask yourself. If you worry that you might be a counter, toucher, or repeater, please talk to your parents about contacting a mental health professional. See chapter 8 for ways to do this.

many steps to the bathroom, brush their teeth so many times, and so on. If one part of the routine is off the slightest bit, they begin all over again.

Some of these may sound like actions of a perfectionist. OCD is different because the person doesn't want to perform the action but feels he or she *must*. Often a perfectionist doesn't mind "perfecting" something.

Thinking back, [I realize that] my OCD with the number forty-seven began after the Flight 800 crash [a 1996 plane crash of a Boeing 747 plane in flight from New York to Paris, France]. I associated the number 7:47 with tragedy and was scared to go to sleep at that time. Ever since then I have been OCD about the number forty-seven.—John, age nineteen

HOARDING

Dennis's bedroom is like a maze. He has almost every paper he has ever written, every magazine he has ever received, and enough newspapers that he could keep a fire going for weeks.

His parents have tried to get him to "straighten up" and throw this stuff out, but he just can't do it. What if he throws something out and then he needs it later? Dennis claims that he knows what's in each pile and can justify why he can't throw away even one newspaper.

Have you ever heard the expression "pack rat"? It is used to describe somebody who cannot throw anything away. A person who is an extreme pack rat may be diagnosed as having OCD in the form of hoarding. People who hoard feel that they must hold on to everything. "Hoarders" cannot throw things away for fear that they will be needed someday or that something bad will happen if they throw something away. Other people hoard because of the memories the objects have for them: They feel that if they get rid of the object, they will lose that part of their life.

Hoarding isn't always classified as OCD. And just because you keep things doesn't make you a hoarder. People save for different reasons. Can you justify why you keep so many things? Is it becoming a danger or health risk? Some people

COULD I BE A HOARDER?*

Do you often:

- Keep objects that you no longer really need?
- Have piles of newspapers or magazines, even if you have already read them?
- Keep random school papers, such as permission slips, daily graded homework assignments, or flyers people were handing out on campus?

*These are just some questions to ask yourself. If you worry that you might be a hoarder, please talk to your parents about contacting a mental health professional. See chapter 8 for ways to do this.

ALCOHOLISM, COMPULSIVE GAMBLING, AND COMPULSIVE SHOPPING

Some people think alcoholism and compulsive gambling or shopping are types of OCD. Although people with these disorders also have anxiety unless they complete their compulsion, there is a difference. With compulsive behaviors, such as compulsive gambling or shopping, the person receives positive reinforcement while performing the behavior: He or she gets enjoyment from the action of drinking, gambling, or shopping. Because of this, the person is more likely to continue the behavior.

With obsessive-compulsive behavior, the person also receives reinforcement. But instead of *gaining* something from performing his or her action, performing the action *gets rid of* the feelings of anxiety. This is called negative reinforcement. Since performing the compulsive behavior helps to rid the anxiety, a person with OCD is also likely to continue this behavior even though the ritual itself usually is not enjoyable.

One form of OCD involves feelings of guilt about having bad thoughts, which can lead to compulsive praying. Photo courtesy of istockphoto.com/ Duncan Walker.

aren't recognized as hoarders for years, until things have really gotten out of hand. For instance, if someone collects empty takeout containers, it might not appear to be a problem until he or she has a whole basement full of them. See chapter 12 for more on hoarding.

OTHER FORMS OF OCD

Do you have a compulsive behavior that hasn't been listed? Over the years, mental health professionals have diagnosed less common forms of OCD. These can cause just as much anxiety as the forms already discussed, but they affect fewer people, so they are not talked about as much in the media.

One type of OCD that is being diagnosed more often is scrupulosity (pronounced SKROO pyuh LOS uh tee). People with this form of OCD get anxious about breaking moral rules or about breaking the rules of their religion. They may pray after they have a bad thought, after they accidentally do something they think is bad or wrong, or after they do something that could be viewed at all negatively. They may pray many times throughout the day, even to the point that it affects their normal life. Although people with scrupulosity may confess their sins repeatedly, they may never feel forgiven, or they may constantly fear that they are going to hell. They may also be compulsively honest to the point of saying things that normally shouldn't be said, such as telling a friend that they dislike his or her new haircut or outfit.

OCD IN THE MIDDLE AGES

During the Middle Ages, people's lives were largely focused on the church. Not surprisingly, there is documentation of people with religious compulsions during this time. They felt guilt for their actions and were compelled to pray constantly. This is probably similar to the type of OCD we now call scrupulosity.

Another type of OCD is called arranging, and it means having to have objects placed just right: corners all lined up, objects arranged symmetrically, and so on. People with this type of OCD feel the urge to arrange so strongly that they must "fix" objects so they are straight or stacked "properly" or in some other type of placement. Obviously, it is not always appropriate to be arranging objects in a room, especially in public.

"Need to Know OCD"

Questions: How long was my shower? Who was on *Oprah* today? What did you have for breakfast? These are questions that, for some reason, you might ask someone for the sole purpose of hearing the answer. People who have a form of OCD called "Need to Know OCD" (NTK-OCD) ask questions for no apparent reason other than to relieve their OCD anxiety.

The types of questions can vary from day to day or hour to hour. Some people with this type of OCD aren't obsessed with the subject matter and don't even necessarily care what the answer is. Often they are merely on a mission to have closure to the question, which helps them get rid of a feeling of doubt. Like hoarders, those with NTK-OCD might write down the information and keep it, in case they need it in the future.[3]

Unwanted Thoughts

Another type of OCD is the kind in which people have unwanted thoughts. They obsess about harming others and fear that they will actually do so. These thoughts include worrying that they will harm a loved one—such as by stabbing—while sleepwalking. They also may worry that these thoughts mean they *want* to perform harmful actions, such as intentionally running someone over with a car. Luckily, performing harmful acts is not a result of OCD. There has never been a reported case of someone with OCD stabbing someone else while sleepwalking.[4] In fact, these people's morals are actually a cause for all the worrying.

Another form of this OCD, which is not often talked about, deals with unwanted sexual thoughts. People might have unwanted or inappropriate thoughts about sex, such as thinking about having sexual relations with family members or animals. They may think that they are perverted or deviant, when in fact it is just the OCD. They really don't have the desire they so fear. These people often perform checks to prove to themselves that their thoughts are false, or they may avoid situations where their thoughts would take place. For instance, a person with a fear of wanting to molest children may avoid any places where children are to ensure that the person won't act on his or her thoughts (even though he or she never would). These people may also pray or try to think good thoughts to help "cancel out" the unwanted thoughts.

In addition, some people with this form of OCD obsess over their sexuality, for example, being afraid they might be homosexual when they are in fact heterosexual or that they might be heterosexual when they are homosexual. They then make sure they don't do things or say things that would lead others to question their sexuality. For example, heterosexual people may think they are "acting gay" or "dressing gay," so they ask others for reassurance that they aren't doing this but are never satisfied with the answers.

CONCLUSION

You may be shocked at how many types of OCD you relate to. It would be surprising if anyone could say he or she has never experienced any of these symptoms! Some are instinctual: We all feel the need to be safe or avoid germs. At a certain point, however, your day-to-day life may start to be affected by your "habits." That is when you might want to ask if it's time to seek help. Read on to find out about the options you have regarding seeing a professional, receiving treatment, and taking medications that are commonly used to help with OCD.

Although the symptoms for OCD can differ dramatically, the symptoms do share in common the following:

- obsessions;
- anxiety;
- ritualizing to decrease the anxiety;
- temporary relief; and
- a repeat of the cycle.

NOTES

1. Tamar E. Chansky, *Freeing Your Child from Obsessive-Compulsive Disorder* (New York: Crown, 2000), 235.

2. N. Fairbrother, S. J. Newth, and S. Rachman, "Mental Pollution: Feelings of Dirtiness Without Physical Contact." *Behaviour Research and Therapy* 43, no. 1 (January 2005): 121–30.

3. William M. Gordon, "Need to Know OCD," *OCD Newsletter* 21, no. 1 (Winter 2007): 4.

4. Karen Cassiday, clinical psychologist and a founding fellow in the Academy of Cognitive Therapy, interview with the author, January 16, 2006.

3 How Do You Get OCD?

A PERSONAL STORY

Mariah, age seventeen

When I was diagnosed with obsessive-compulsive disorder at the age of fourteen, my psychiatrist described the disorder to me as "being trapped inside a small room with a locked door, no lights, and hundreds of flies buzzing around your head." That analogy made perfect sense to me; that was how I had felt my entire life.

After I was diagnosed, everything made so much more sense to me. I finally knew why I felt like I needed to turn the radio on and off seventeen times, or blink in the mirror for twenty-one seconds before going to bed. OCD had been affecting my everyday life, and I didn't even know it. It became difficult for me to have conversations at school because I said, "Thank you, sorry, sorry, thank you" after everything I said. I distracted other students in class with my loud breathing patterns, and my friends and family became increasingly annoyed with me when I asked them to repeat words seven times. All of my patterns seemed logical to me, no matter how inconvenient they were.

Can you remember back to your first OCD episode? You might not even remember a time before you had it. In the movie *The Aviator*, Howard Hughes has flashbacks of his mother stressing the importance of staying clean. Do you ever blame your parents for some of your behaviors? If it didn't come from them, where did it come from? And why does one person get it, but someone else doesn't?

OCD is now thought to be a biological disorder. Rather than the way you were raised (your nurturing) being the culprit, it's probably due more to your biology (nature). However, an

> ## HOLES IN THE HEAD
>
> While today's therapists would not use a drill as a form of treatment for mental illness, scientists have found evidence of drilling in skulls of humans in the Stone Age. They believe these ancient people drilled holes in the skulls of those who were mentally ill to release "the demons" that were believed to cause their mental illness. There are records of mental illness affecting the Babylonians, Native American tribes, and other ancient peoples. Some Native Americans thought mental illness was caused by evil spirits. To rid the body of this evil, a shaman performed a dance and a chant. This ritual would also remove creatures, such as snakes or toads that only the shaman could see, from the body.[1]

individual does seem to have a higher chance of getting OCD if a parent had it as well—roughly 25 percent of children with OCD have someone in their immediate family with OCD.[2]

Here's the science behind it: Each of us is born with an equal number of genes from our mother and our father. These genes determine, for example, the color of our hair and whether it is curly or straight, and what color our eyes will be. Just as physical traits are carried down through the genes, so are mental traits.

You may wonder if you got OCD because your parents performed a certain action and then you repeated it—for example, if you saw your dad always touch a light switch four times after turning it off, you did, too. Scientists have found, however, that although some parents with OCD have a child with OCD, the type of OCD the child has is often different. For example, a checker might have a child who ends up being a counter. In addition, if people got OCD because of the actions they copied from parents, there would probably be more cases of siblings with the same type of OCD. You don't have OCD because your mom made you wash your hands before dinner or check that you had your homework in your schoolbag each morning. It's also not because your parents didn't love you enough or spend enough time with you, or because they spent too much time with you . . . you get the idea. In a nutshell, one way you "get" OCD is from genetics—and for that, you can thank Mom and Dad.

PANDAS

Another type of OCD occurs as a result of a strep infection. Although strep is contagious, it does not always cause OCD. This type of OCD is called pediatric autoimmune neuropsychiatric disorders associated with streptococcal infections (PANDAS). Children who have this type of OCD start to get obsessions and compulsions abruptly, rather than over time. Before they were exposed to strep, they had few, if any, OCD-type symptoms; after having a specific type of strep infection, children diagnosed with PANDAS are moderately to severely bothered by obsessions and compulsions. This is not something to worry about the next time you have strep; it is an unusual circumstance, and it is almost always diagnosed in young children. Although there are more than forty different strains of strep infection,[3] only a few cause a PANDAS-type reaction. Scientists have found that this happens to some people and not to others, and it happens more often to children with a genetic predisposition to OCD.[4] They have not yet discovered a way to detect this in advance.

Physiologically what happens in PANDAS is that the immune cells that should be attacking the infection attack the basal ganglia in the brain instead, causing obsessions and compulsions. These obsessions and compulsions may become less severe for a while and then return again if the person becomes ill with another strep infection. In addition, the person may have some of the following symptoms:

- tics;
- nightmares;
- uncontrollable movements of the arms, legs, or face;
- hyperactivity;
- trouble sleeping; and
- difficulty with handwriting.[5]

Neurological symptoms, such as tics, hyperactivity, or Sydenham's chorea (a less common but more extreme condition that makes walking and other movements difficult), always accompany OCD from PANDAS.[6]

As with the more typical kind of OCD, there is no cure, but the same treatments—cognitive behavioral therapy (CBT) and medication—work for PANDAS. Since strep can cause a flare-up of symptoms, any strep infection should be treated with antibiotics by a doctor (antibiotics are normally used to treat strep in people without OCD from PANDAS as well). Sometimes the OCD caused by PANDAS responds well to antibiotics, and no therapy or OCD medication is needed. To get an accurate diagnosis of PANDAS, you need to have a strep test that is read after forty-eight hours (called a throat culture of group A Beta-hemolytic strep) and a blood test (anti-DNAse B and antistreptolysin [ASO] titers).[7]

If you think you may have this type of OCD, it might be good to talk to your parents about your medical history. They, along with your doctor, may be able to determine if and when you've ever had strep.

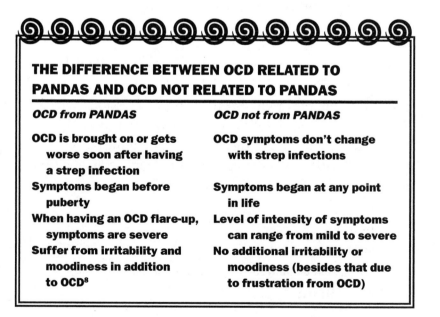

THE DIFFERENCE BETWEEN OCD RELATED TO PANDAS AND OCD NOT RELATED TO PANDAS

OCD from PANDAS	OCD not from PANDAS
OCD is brought on or gets worse soon after having a strep infection	OCD symptoms don't change with strep infections
Symptoms began before puberty	Symptoms began at any point in life
When having an OCD flare-up, symptoms are severe	Level of intensity of symptoms can range from mild to severe
Suffer from irritability and moodiness in addition to OCD[8]	No additional irritability or moodiness (besides that due to frustration from OCD)

ASK YOUR FAMILY QUESTIONS

As you read this book, you might want to talk to your parents and relatives about your medical and social history. Questions you might ask include:

- What was I like as a baby?
- Was I anxious?
- Did I have ear infections a lot?
- Did I have strep as a child?

Children with OCD often get sick with such ailments as ear infections more frequently than children without OCD. Scientists have found that conditions one has as a child, such as delayed walking and talking or having allergies, may be the result of differences in the brain and occur more often in children who are later diagnosed with OCD.[9]

You may also want to ask questions about your OCD, as well as about your relatives' medical histories (if they're willing to share). These questions might include:

- When did you first notice my OCD?
- Did it start suddenly or slowly over time?
- Does anyone else in our family have OCD?

NOTES

1. Deborah Kent, *Snake Pits, Talking Cures, & Magic Bullets: A History of Mental Illness* (Brookfield, CT: Twenty-First Century Books, 2003), 16–18.

2. Aureen Pinto Wagner, *What to Do When Your Child Has Obsessive-Compulsive Disorder: Strategies and Solutions* (Rochester, NY: Lighthouse Press, 2002), 106.

3. Karen Cassiday, clinical psychologist and a founding fellow in the Academy of Cognitive Therapy, written correspondence with the author, January 22, 2008.

4. Wagner, *What to Do*, 104.

5. The Children's Center for OCD and Anxiety, "Pediatric Autoimmune Neuropsychiatric Disorders Associated with Strep (PANDAS): A subtype of OCD, www.worrywisekids.org/anxiety/pandas.html (accessed April 9, 2008).

6. Cassiday.

7. Phoebe Moore, PhD (clinical psychologist), emailed on April 1, 2008.

8. Cassiday.

9. Mitzi Waltz, *Obsessive-Compulsive Disorder: Help for Children* (Sebatopol, CA: O'Reilly & Associates, Inc., 2000), 9.

4

What Is Going On in My Brain?

Harry didn't feel as if he was getting anywhere.

OCD can make you feel like you're stuck in one spot. Illustration by John Aardema.

The human brain weighs a whopping 3 pounds. But what exactly goes on in there? Let's do a quick biology review.

There are three main parts to the brain: the cerebrum, the cerebellum, and the brain stem. The cerebrum, which makes up most of the brain, is the focus of this chapter. The cerebellum is a potato-shaped section of the brain involved with coordination and processing information. The brain stem is responsible for controlling the heartbeat and breathing and for regulating sleeping, arousal, motivation, and reward. It is also the checkpoint between other parts of the brain and the spinal cord. It includes the midbrain, the pons, and the medulla.

THE CEREBRUM

The wrinkled surface of the cerebrum is called the cerebral cortex. It is a thin rind made up of nerve cells. The cerebral cortex has many jobs: It is important for problem solving, thinking, planning, learning, remembering, and more. It is divided into four different lobes: the frontal, parietal, temporal (one half on each side of the cerebrum), and occipital.

Here is a breakdown of the four lobes:

- *Frontal lobe*: Near the front of the brain; involved in speech, emotion, movement, judgment, motivation, problem solving, impulse control, and planning. The orbital frontal cortex, mentioned later, is in this part of the cerebral cortex. It allows you to imagine what might be the outcomes of your actions, and it is important in suppressing behaviors that you know aren't good for you.
- *Parietal lobe*: Behind the frontal lobe; involved in sensations such as pain, temperature, touch, pressure, and our ability to attend to visual-spatial orientation.
- *Temporal lobe*: Below the frontal and parietal lobes and next to the occipital lobe; involved in hearing, speech, smell, taste, emotion, some memory, and some vision.
- *Occipital lobe*: Near the back of the brain; involved in vision.

There are parts located in the center of the brain (part of the forebrain) that affect OCD, such as the thalamus and the basal

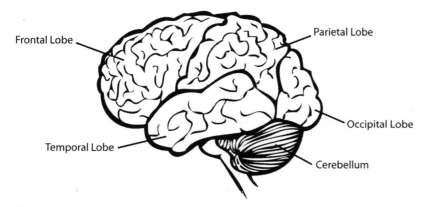

Frontal Lobe

Parietal Lobe

Occipital Lobe

Temporal Lobe

Cerebellum

The cerebral cortex can be divided into four lobes. (Also shown is the cerebellum.) Illustration by John Aardema.

ganglia. The thalamus passes messages (such as sensations) from the spinal cord to the cerebrum. The basal ganglia, a network of fibers, help with processing motor movement (like moving your arms and legs). One structure that is part of the basal ganglia (that will be mentioned in relation to OCD) is the caudate nucleus. It allows us to select and use the appropriate action for a task.

WHAT THIS HAS TO DO WITH OCD

There is a lot happening all the time in your brain. Scientists have found that in those with OCD, other actions are also occurring. When working properly, your brain is like a well-oiled machine—one part passing on messages to another. Your brain works with your whole body to help you ice skate, watch a sunset, and listen to your favorite song. Of course, to do any action involves many processes that need to work together like a factory assembly line. If one part is not functioning the way it should, the whole process can go haywire.

Looking at positron emission tomography (PET) scans, scientists have been able to see that parts of the brain—including the caudate nucleus in the basal ganglia and orbital cortex in the frontal lobe—are overactive in people with OCD. The orbital cortex sends more messages than it should to the basal ganglia's caudate nucleus. These parts are not functioning

41

PETs AND MRIs

By the 1980s scientists had solid evidence that OCD may be related to neurobiology. PET scans and magnetic resonance imaging (MRI) revealed that parts of the brain are more active in patients with OCD. Once they learned about the differences in the brain activity of those with OCD, scientists and doctors began to find ways to treat it.

the way they should. This can cause compulsions. You can "work" your brain to better control your OCD.

VOLUNTARY AND INVOLUNTARY ACTIONS

Your brain controls both your voluntary and involuntary actions. Voluntary action occurs in such things as kicking a ball

When I experience an episode, it is like an alarm that is short-circuited and will not shut off.—Dieter, age thirty-nine

or swallowing your food. Involuntary actions would be actions that occur automatically, such as breathing and digesting food.

This is important to understand because when you have OCD, your brain is *voluntarily* telling your body to perform your compulsions. It is not a reflex or something it really has to do. *You can regain control over what your body is doing. The compulsions are total mind games that can be stopped.* This requires time and effort, and will be uncomfortable to do—very uncomfortable—but less uncomfortable than having your OCD controlling you. This is why getting professional help from a trained therapist is strongly suggested.

NEUROTRANSMITTERS

It's not just the physical parts of the brain that are involved in OCD; there are also chemicals that play a major role. Neurotransmitters are the chemicals the nerve cells in your brain use to communicate with one another. They get from one neuron to the next by crossing synaptic clefts, or spaces. Some of the more common neurotransmitters include adrenaline, which produces the "fight or flight" reaction to stressful situations, as well as endorphins, which help control pain and reward.

Having an insufficient amount of the neurotransmitter serotonin is thought to be related to having OCD. Serotonin plays a role in sleep, mood, and body temperature. Other neurotransmitters thought to be related to OCD are dopamine and norepinephrine. Dopamine affects movement, thinking, emotion, and the feeling of being rewarded by something a person enjoys. OCD medications and CBT can change the release levels of these neurotransmitters.

TREATMENTS AND THE BRAIN

There are many treatments available that help alter the brain activity of people with OCD. Medications such as selective serotonin reuptake inhibitors (SSRIs) work on the synapses to help keep the neurotransmitter serotonin at the right level. They do this by prolonging the activity of the serotonin signal that

THE STORY OF PHINEAS GAGE

In 1848 Phineas Gage was working on the railroad when his 13½-pound tamping iron, not properly packed with sand, exploded, piercing through his jaw and out the top of his head. Surprisingly, he survived the injury. But he was different. He no longer got along with the other workers, becoming rude, impatient, and swearing frequently. Doctors believe his frontal lobe was damaged from his injury. This case helped doctors see firsthand the effect of injury to a specific part of the brain.

TALK LIKE A NEUROPSYCHIATRY EXPERT

ECT: electroconvulsive therapy—a type of therapy that uses electric currents that cause a seizure in the brain, which helps in treating severe mental illness

MRI: magnetic resonance imaging—a medical imaging technique that takes images of the body using magnets and radio waves

PET: positron emission tomography—a medical imaging technique that takes images of biochemical activity in the body using a radioactive chemical (called a tracer) that is injected into the bloodstream

SSRIs: selective serotonin reuptake inhibitors—medications that help regulate serotonin levels in the brain, often prescribed to help treat OCD

nerve cells use to communicate with one another, potentially overcoming the deficiency in serotonin that causes certain aspects of OCD.

In severe cases of OCD, doctors might use electroconvulsive therapy, better known as ECT. In ECT, electrodes are attached to the scalp. Currents of electricity are charged through the electrodes, causing shocks to the brain that cause nerve cells to release massive amounts of their neurotransmitters. Although this may sound painful, the patient is put under anesthesia and doesn't feel any pain. This procedure is not often used but is remarkably effective when it is.

Other people who are unable to live a normal, functioning life may end up getting psychosurgery, in which a tiny electrode is implanted in the brain. A battery pack is attached to the electrode, and the system can be used to interrupt the signals that are promoting compulsive behavior. (Psychosurgery is something of a "last resort" that would be thoroughly discussed with the patient and agreed upon by both the patient and the doctor as the best treatment.)

5 Other Mental Disorders

You may have seen movies, television specials, or books or magazine articles about people with mental disorders with some of the same symptoms as OCD—such as attention-deficit/hyperactivity disorder, social phobia, specific phobias, and schizophrenia—and wondered how they are different from OCD. Here is a brief description of these other mental disorders and how they differ from OCD.

ADHD

ADHD is a condition in which an individual has a great deal of difficulty focusing on tasks and/or experiences high levels of impulsivity or hyperactivity. People with ADHD may have trouble keeping their attention on a task, which can impact them at school, at home, and at work. They may be easily distracted or seem forgetful. (A complete list of diagnostic criteria for ADHD can be found in *DSM-IV-TR*, listed in the bibliography at the end of the book.)

In contrast, while some people with OCD may be forgetful or unable to focus on a task, the difference is that they are often distracted by an obsession or concentrating on completing a compulsion (often a mental ritual). For example, a high school student who has a compulsion to avoid writing the number three might fail to complete a timed math test. This is not due to an inability to concentrate on the test, but rather on the student's obsession with a particular number.

SOCIAL PHOBIA

Like OCD, social phobia is an anxiety disorder. People with social phobia fear embarrassing themselves in social situations. Some people with social phobia feel shy all the time; others just feel anxiety in certain situations, such as when answering questions in class or hanging out at a party.

People with OCD might look like they have social phobia if they avoid social situations so people won't see them performing their ritualistic behavior. The difference is that people with true social phobia have a fear of a normal situation that should not cause embarrassment, such as worrying about the cashier seeing their hands tremble as they purchase something at the mall.

SPECIFIC PHOBIAS

Specific phobias are also an anxiety disorder. What are some differences between having a phobia and having OCD? In a specific phobia, one type of object or situation causes extreme fear, such as a fear of snakes or a fear of small places. The fears can seem to make sense because the person is afraid of things that are understandably feared; however, the person has a more severe fearful reaction than necessary. People who have phobias know their fears are irrational or out of proportion, but they can't help their reaction. Sometimes even something related to their phobia, such as a photo or drawing of the feared object or situation, can make them feel afraid.

The difference between having a phobia and having OCD is that a phobia is specific: The person has a fear of that one type of situation, such as a fear of heights, a fear of spiders, or a fear of small spaces. With OCD, the obsessions and compulsions may change across the person's lifetime. The person may have a fear of contamination, and then, years later, suffer from the need to check objects. A person with OCD usually also has multiple obsessions and compulsions at the same time.

Another difference is that OCD has that second awful component: the compulsive behaviors or actions. With a

PHOBIAS THAT LOOK LIKE OCD

Below is a short list of various phobias people have. You may see that there are some that resemble obsessions people with OCD have.

- arsonphobia or pyrophobia: fear of fire
- bacteriophobia or microbiophobia: fear of germs (bacteria or microbes)
- bromidrosiphobia: fear of body odor
- cleptophobia or kleptophobia: fear of stealing
- emetophobia: fear of vomiting
- helminthophobia: fear of infestation of worms (as in meats)
- homophobia: fear of homosexuality or becoming homosexual
- numerophobia: fear of numbers
- rhypophobia or misophobia: fear of filth
- satanophobia: fear of Satan
- scatophobia: fear of fecal matter
- triskaidekaphobia: fear of the number thirteen

phobia, the person often just avoids situations that cause fear, but someone with OCD feels compelled to perform particular actions in an attempt to calm their fears.

There are a plethora of phobias. Like the different types of OCD, some may be surprising (such as hippopotomonstrosesquippedaliophobia—a fear of long words). Phobias are severe fears that cause anxiety. Like OCD, phobias are a medical condition with a spectrum of levels of severity.

SCHIZOPHRENIA

Schizophrenia affects people in ways that may appear similar to OCD. Schizophrenia is a psychotic disorder, which means the person suffers from hallucinations, delusions, or illusions. People with schizophrenia usually develop symptoms around their late teens. Many have delusions and hallucinations they think are real, such as hearing voices and seeing images that don't exist. This is different from OCD because those with OCD don't actually see things that are nonexistent; they just feel they can't trust what they've seen. People with OCD usually also know their mind is playing games but can't risk ignoring their compulsions, whereas people with schizophrenia are unaware that their mind is playing tricks on them. Schizophrenia involves mainly the neurotransmitters dopamine and glutamate, and, like OCD, it may be a genetic disorder.

CONCLUSION

While the above disorders may seem to have something in common with OCD, they are not all part of the same category of mental disorder as OCD. *DSM-IV-TR*, the "bible" of mental disorders, categorizes OCD as an anxiety disorder. We will discuss other related disorders in detail in chapter 12, but other anxiety disorders include panic attacks, agoraphobia, specific phobias, generalized anxiety disorder (GAD), and post-traumatic stress disorder. Sometimes these disorders also occur in people with OCD. Some of the medications that are used to help treat OCD are also used to treat other anxiety disorders.

OCD WITH POOR INSIGHT

Although most people with OCD realize that their mind is playing tricks on them, people with one type of OCD—known as OCD with poor insight—do not know it's all in their mind. They don't realize that their obsessions and compulsions are irrational.

6

Effects of OCD on School and Work

A PERSONAL STORY

John, age nineteen

The first time I started obsessing must have been when I was in sixth grade, weird stuff [like] having to shoot basketball hoops from both sides an equal number of times, having to go to bed at certain times, big fear of number forty-seven, and not being able to wear certain clothes and stuff. However, for me, when my OCD got real bad and I didn't realize that was what I had [was] in freshman year of high school: Some kids got kicked out for smoking marijuana and I thought it was my fault and it ruined my freshman year because I felt so anxious by it all.

My status at this point is up in the air, from an OCD point it is pretty bad. I have really isolated myself from my friends and I am having a hard time. However, from a therapeutic standpoint I feel as though I have finally reached the point necessary to truly embrace CBT [cognitive behavioral therapy] and take positive steps toward achieving complete recovery. I just finished my freshman year in college, and what I was doing was doing rituals here and there to avoid the anxiety and then going out and having fun; however, this "strategy" of doing a little here and there backfired and now I am back to square one. However, I have now realized that a full-on CBT approach is the only way out of this stuff.

I am now seeing a psychiatrist and am currently on medication. Back at school in about March I had my OCD turning point and got really bad and went to the school counselor there. They put me on Luvox and I got it up to 150 mg until I came home. I started seeing a psychiatrist here and she has put me on Prozac. I am at 30 mg and will go up to 40 mg and see where I stand. I am also supplementing the medication with Inositol (vitamin B) and am taking omega-3. [Author's Note: Do not supplement medication with vitamins without the okay from your psychiatrist and/or medical doctor.]

My condition has gotten worse, however I feel like I have never reached the point that I am willing to fight my OCD 100 percent, so I have dedicated this summer to really fighting the good fight.

Many people with OCD think they can take care of their condition on their own. Others think it's not a big deal and that they are doing fine without treatment. Maybe your OCD impacts your life, but you're not aware of it.

SCHOOL

Some people have compulsions that cause them to be late for school every morning. Maybe they have to brush their teeth just right, walk the correct number of paces to the bus stop, have their hair just so, or scrub themselves until they feel "clean enough."

Chances are, as they arrive late to first period, they don't explain to their teacher their reason for being late. It might seem less embarrassing to lie or just accept the detention slip.

Some people with OCD have difficulty getting enough sleep because they spend too long working on homework as a result of their compulsion(s): sharpening their pencil "just right," reading the same sentence four times, and so on. What are some consequences of that? They might wake up unrested and be cranky or late for school. They might not have the energy to give school their complete attention. This can become a vicious circle that gets progressively worse.

AUTHOR'S STORY

A Simple OCD Math Lesson

As a teacher myself, I have had students who are chronically late for class. Since I want them to start off the day by jump-starting their brains, I assign an important task within those first ten minutes. Let's do the simple math: If a student is late to class ten minutes, let's say only two out of the five days a week, how much school is that student actually missing? That would mean twenty minutes a week, one hour and twenty minutes a month, and twelve hours a year! Twelve hours less of school a year. How much of school time is that in a lifetime? If the student's disorder started when he or she was ten and it went through just to high school, that would be ninety-six hours—or *thirteen* school days— lost. Don't you think it puts that student at a disadvantage?

OCD can directly affect schoolwork as well. If the type of OCD prevents a person from writing certain words or numbers, it can make it impossible to complete an assignment or get the right answers on a homework assignment or test. For example, someone who feels that writing the number three on a test would cause harm to his or her family would get all of the problems wrong that contain the number three. Obviously, grades are often affected by OCD.

School can be torture for people with contamination issues. Bathrooms must be avoided, public desks cause anxiety, and wearing a school-issued swimsuit is a nightmare. You can imagine how these things can influence the day-to-day life of someone with these issues. OCD can even cause people to not eat lunch if they believe the cafeteria food is contaminated.

Students with OCD often end up missing school. If you are worried about graduating with your class, there might be accommodations that can be made. You might be able to graduate with the class and then make up the missing courses.

A PERSONAL STORY
Claire, age nineteen

School has never been a daunting task for me, but I would say it's not a piece of cake either. When it comes to reading books, I tend to have trouble because I often reread sentences. So if I do not understand a sentence, I will logically reread the sentence for a better understanding. However, even if I understand the meaning the second time around, I have convinced myself somehow that I do not in fact comprehend the sentence; therefore, I must reread the sentence again and again. What is even more frustrating is when I clearly understand a sentence or passage the first time around, but my brain tricks itself into believing I do not understand. It seems as if my brain is in denial of its abilities to complete a task successfully the first time.

Other than the repeating of sentences, I really enjoy school because it's my foundation in life. I know how to write papers, talk to teachers, and take tests. I guess school is my anchor because it provides a predictable order in my life. I'm a combination of a Type A personality and easygoing kid. It's quite an oxymoron. With OCD I like to be organized and I'm known to make several lists of things I need to accomplish. I'm not an extreme case like Monk, but I would rather say I have a mild case of OCD.

Accommodations can be made in school to help students with OCD, such as getting to take tests in a small-group setting. Photo courtesy of istockphoto.com/Soubrette.

HOW TO GET A RESTFUL SLEEP

Did you know that when you haven't had enough sleep it can make you have more or stronger OCD "attacks"? So can a change in your sleep pattern. Here are some tips for getting a restful sleep:

- Get the recommended amount of sleep for your age.
- Go to bed only when you're tired.
- Don't read or watch TV in bed.
- If you can't sleep, get up and do something boring, like reading a textbook—avoid screens (TV and computer).
- Drink a glass of warm milk.
- Avoid caffeine, nicotine, alcohol, and sugar after lunchtime and for the rest of the day. (Obviously nicotine and alcohol should always be avoided if you're underage.)
- Be consistent as to what time you go to bed and wake up daily (even on weekends).
- Avoid eating foods right before bed that give you digestive trouble.
- Don't nap during the day.
- Journal before bed and get all your thoughts and worries out of your head.
- Soak in a hot bath for twenty minutes or so before you plan to go to bed.

A PERSONAL STORY
Claire, age nineteen

Some things I've used in the past [to stop rereading compulsively] may be telling one of my parents that I'm rereading. And they distract me for a while by talking to me, then I pick up the book again. Also I tell myself, "Claire, you don't need to catch every detail, just the basics." When I was in high school and crunched for time to meet a deadline that involved reading a book and writing a paper, my mom would say, "Skim the rest of the book." But I could never just "skim" the book; that wasn't the way I completed assignments. I had to read the book from start to finish, then spend a good amount of time writing the paper. I used to be jealous of my older brother because sometimes he never even picked up the book and still received an A on the paper. With all assignments, I have to work at it. It's like a puzzle, each piece at a time. But my problem (more like challenge) is spending too much time on one puzzle and becoming stressed when the next one comes along. Tests can also be very challenging for me because I can spend too much time on one particular question. That's why I hated the ACT, time restrictions for each sections and not enough time for the reading section. My classmates in high school always knew I'd be the last one to finish a test. It sort of became a joke after a while.

There are also alternatives to receiving your high school diploma. If you don't graduate, after the age of eighteen you may take the General Educational Development (GED) test. The GED is a battery of pass/fail tests with questions on English, history, math, and reading. Many jobs require a high school diploma or GED. If this is of interest to you, your high school can give you more information.

If you plan to get your GED and still want to attend college, you will need to look into whether your college of choice accepts a GED. You will still need to meet the other requirements of the college application, such as writing an essay.

Laws That Could Help You

Unfortunately, many students with disorders and health conditions end up dropping out of high school or not attending college. By law, teachers and administrators (both high school and college) are required to make accommodations for students with "special needs." Although that term may scare you, having OCD may require you to have special accommodations made.

You need to let someone at your high school or college know about your OCD. You could start by telling your teacher or professor, a counselor, or, if you are in high school, your principal. One of these professionals should be able to point you in the direction of the appropriate person in the school to help you out.

504 Plans

In order to receive special accommodations, you will probably be put on a 504 Plan. The term 504 Plan refers to Section 504 of the Rehabilitation Act of 1973. This act requires that students who have disabilities receive the education and accommodations they need. A 504 Plan is a document written by the parents, teachers, and school administration. The disability may be physical, such as being in a wheelchair, or mental, such as having OCD. The accommodations the student needs as a result of his or her condition are written into the 504 Plan. This makes teachers aware of the student's needs so they can be sure to meet them accordingly. This plan is also useful for students in college.

A 504 Plan allows accommodations to be made and outlines those accommodations. Maybe you need more time on tests because you have trouble writing without starting over and erasing. Maybe you have trouble selecting option B on multiple-choice tests. Whatever your situation is, you need to be open and honest with the people working out your 504 Plan so that your schoolwork doesn't suffer.

Great IDEAs

Sometimes an Individualized Education Program (IEP) is written instead of a 504 Plan. This document, which is more structured about modifications that are needed and has goals for you as well, is mandated by the Individuals with Disabilities Education Act (IDEA). IDEA is a federal law that ensures that students with disabilities are given the proper education.

Public schools are required by law to follow IDEA and make modifications as needed, but private schools (including colleges) don't have to follow the laws requiring special accommodations. This might be something to realize if you are in a private school and are not receiving the services you need.

Accomodations and Modifications

As you might have encountered, there are people who don't understand OCD. You may have a teacher who is not willing to make modifications. It often isn't up to him or her; you need to find the person who works with special needs and see what the policy is.

You should realize that you may not be able to work around every aspect of your OCD, but any accommodation can help. Some of the following suggestions come from Dr. Tamar Chansky's book *Freeing Your Child from Obsessive-Compulsive Disorder*. Although it is written for parents of children with OCD, it has great information about the school setting and is reader-friendly. Here is a list of different strategies that may work for you, depending on your needs (some you can do yourself; others your teacher or professor would have to set up):

- having a second set of textbooks: one for home, one for school
- being given a limited number of bathroom passes throughout the day
- reducing the amount of work
- obtaining a time limit for assignments
- typing work instead of writing it by hand
- having someone else write lecture notes and getting a copy of those notes
- dictating thoughts to someone else
- circling answers for bubble tests and having the answers transferred to the bubble sheet for you
- breaking large projects into smaller chunks with deadlines—once done, not being able to change that part
- having standardized and classroom tests be untimed

- ◎ **taking tests in a quiet area in a small-group setting**
- ◎ **being given short-answer tests instead of multiple choice**
- ◎ **having study hall first period**
- ◎ **having PE last period**
- ◎ **getting clothes and schoolwork ready the night before**
- ◎ **being given extra time to get from class to class**
- ◎ **getting to leave class to take breaks or when feeling anxious**
- ◎ **being allowed to ritualize only for the length of a song**
- ◎ **limiting the amount of caffeine in the afternoon and evening**
- ◎ **keeping the nighttime routine the same[1]**

In all honesty, others may notice that you are getting "special treatment." You may want to think ahead about how you will handle this. If good friends are asking, you may want to tell them what's going on. They may be able to help you in class either by sharing their notes with you or helping you lower your anxiety when a compulsion is coming on.

If you've started CBT or ERP (see chapter 9), you might wonder where school fits into this. Exam time can be hard. If you are taking a major test, such as the ACT, SAT, or final exams in college, you probably would still want modifications. Trying to concentrate on the test and do ERP at the same time might just be too difficult. Talk to your therapist about what you should do. Often your therapist can also help your teachers and school counselors decide which accommodations are best for you during school.

Not everyone will be understanding about your needs for accommodating your OCD; it is a misunderstood disorder. Instead of referring to it as OCD, you may prefer to call it (or have better results calling it) an anxiety disorder.[2]

Returning to School after Hospitalization

If you have been in the hospital because of your OCD, it is best to decide ahead of time what you want to tell your friends and teachers who don't know about your hospitalization. Some people find that it's easiest to just tell the truth, explaining to others that they went away to a special program where they learned how to overcome their anxiety, or OCD. Other people prefer to keep things more private, telling others that they took a vacation or visited a sick relative. Choose whatever feels comfortable to you and helps you be most comfortable when you return to school. You don't owe others an explanation, but you should realize that people may ask you about your absence.

College

Although many people with OCD have higher than average intelligence,[3] many worry about going to college. College can be stressful even for those without this disorder; with OCD it sometimes seems as if it would be impossible: harder classes, sharing a dorm, less sleep. The key word is here is *seem*.

People with OCD *can* go to college and succeed. Again, getting therapy is important, and some modifications may need to be made. Please realize, however, that you will not be able to have modifications made for every class that you take. At some point you're going to need to face your OCD head-on and try to treat it. In the meantime, here are some ways to help you be successful in college.

First, it is important to pick a college that can meet your needs. You will want to keep this in mind while you are deciding where to go. A good person to contact at the colleges you are interested in is the disability counselor. He or she can tell you the percentage of students with disabilities who are registered there (realize, however, that a lot of students with disabilities never tell anyone) and what types of accommodations the college can make.

The size of the college may make a difference to you. Bigger colleges usually have very large freshman classes. Some classes might involve lectures twice a week with hundreds of students and then a small group once a week. This might sound appealing because you can blend in with the crowd, but it can be difficult because there's no one looking out for you.

Smaller colleges often have smaller class sizes. Your professors will probably know your name and will be more willing to work with you personally.

Most schools require you to stay in a residence hall your freshman year, although some schools waive this requirement for students with disabilities. If not, you may be able to arrange to live in a single room instead of having a roommate or roommates.

When you are registering for classes, you'll want to think about your class load. Each semester, try to pick a class or two that seem a little easier so you're not overwhelmed. College classes can be quite different from high school classes. Some schools offer priority registration for those with disabilities so they can be sure to get a schedule that works for them.

Here's something to watch for when choosing how many classes to take: In order to be considered a full-time student, you usually need to take twelve credit hours a semester. If your parents' insurance covers you because you are a full-time student, you need to make sure you are taking enough classes. You can ask a disability counselor whether you can have this waived because of your condition.

YOU GOTTA READ THIS!

***The Thought That Counts: A Firsthand Account of One Teenager's Experience with Obsessive-Compulsive Disorder*, by Jared Douglas Kant with Martin Franklin, PhD, and Linda Wasmer Andrews**

Want to hear about the experiences of a teenager with OCD? Each chapter in this book is divided into two parts. First, Jared Douglas Kant—a checker, counter, cleaner, and sufferer of unwanted thoughts—shares his personal experience with having OCD in a section titled "My Story." He tells about dating, school life, and ways he found to help him to de-stress. What's neat about this book is that it isn't just an autobiography. The other section of each chapter is called "The Big Picture." Here, you will learn more general information, such as questions to ask your therapist and how OCD affects your home and school life.

You may find that a course you've signed up for is just too difficult. This is common with all college students. Don't get discouraged! Sometimes the timing's just wrong. Don't give up your dream career because you are doing poorly in a course you have to take. It happens to lots of people—even those without OCD. You may want to drop the course if you can, so the grade won't even appear in your records. (There's usually a set amount of time from the beginning of the semester when you can add or drop a class without being penalized.) You can always try again another semester. It could even be that the professor is not a good match for you and you need to switch sections. You can usually find someone who knows the personalities of the professors and can give you a heads-up on who would be right for you.

As in high school, accommodations can often be made to help you in classes, including alternatives to tests and more time to complete assignments and exams.

You should also know that many people end up transferring colleges after the first year and sometimes even the first semester. Maybe the school just isn't a good fit for you. A community college is a great place to start college or transfer to while you are deciding on a four-year school you might want to go to.

Realize that college might be the first time you have had to take care of yourself all on your own. It is fine to still have your parents involved, but eventually you will need to speak up for yourself. You know what you need, so try to take care of questions you have for yourself.

This is also a good time to start taking charge of ordering and picking up your own medications, if you have any. It is much easier if you find a psychiatrist nearby who can prescribe your medications instead of relying on one back home. Often the college's health center can prescribe medicines and offer a discount.

Finally, be sure to keep in touch with friends and family, whether by phone, letters, e-mail, or text messaging. College can be a whole different world, and it can be comforting to hear from a good friend.

College is a challenge for most freshmen, even those without disabilities. Having the freedom to choose when to study, when

College can present new challenges, but having some strategies in place can help. Photo courtesy of istockphoto.com/YinYang.

to go to sleep, and what to eat may be difficult at first. The stress of college (and lack of sleep) may even cause OCD flare-ups. A counselor should be able to explain to you how the school's mental health services work.

To find a good OCD therapist or psychiatrist near your school, visit the OCF online (www.ocfoundation.org, click "Find a Doctor") and its regional affiliates (on the same Web site, click "OC Foundation Affiliates"), or the Anxiety Disorder Association of America (www.adaa.org, click "Find a Therapist"). Student health center therapists are usually trained

When I was in college I would scout out the cleanest bathroom. It was on the sixth floor of the engineering building. It was very difficult to have a social life. When the OCD was at its worst, I even laid out important papers and sprayed them with disinfectant because I thought they were contaminated with HIV. Afterward, I would let them sit in the sun until they were dried.—Dieter, age thirty-nine

to help with short-term adjustment difficulties and are not prepared to provide CBT, which is known to best help OCD.[4]

Vocational School and Other Options

If you are planning on going to vocational school, there are transition-to-work programs that help to place people with disabilities into jobs that work for them. This is especially helpful if your OCD would prevent you from working at many types of jobs.

If you are unsure what career path you want to take and feel that your OCD will limit your options, try going to your public library or a nearby community college to get information about what options you have. Both places may have someone willing to discuss career choices that are right for you. You should also consider seeing an OCD therapist. Most people with OCD can expect to overcome their symptoms with proper treatment, making almost any career possible.

WORK

If you're out of school (either because you graduated or you were not able to complete school) or have an after-school job, you might think your life is not affected by your OCD. Maybe it isn't—but maybe it is. Take this quick quiz:

◎ **Do you ever recount money or objects several times, even though the number is always the same?**

> **Oftentimes I just wouldn't show up somewhere rather than be late as a result of the OCD. I was so overwhelmed with distress and anxiety that I couldn't bear to face anyone. Also, if I was running late because an OCD episode was holding me back, I often would just cancel plans, stay home from work, or not show up somewhere. I just figured that whatever the consequences were, they didn't compare to how I was feeling as a result of the OCD.—Dieter, age thirty-nine**

- Do you have to arrange things on a shelf or counter to be "just right"?
- Do you wash your hands after shaking hands with someone or after touching everyday objects?
- Do you worry excessively that you've said or done something inappropriate?
- Do you save every e-mail, written document, and voice mail you receive in case you'll need them later?
- Do you fear you'll harm someone, so you choose not to work in positions where you would need to interact with other people?

Answering "yes" to these questions alone does not guarantee that your OCD is affecting your work, but they are

> In the early years of OCD (I first began to experience symptoms at age twenty), work was very difficult to deal with. I was always exhausted from having the OCD control every aspect of my life. Therefore, since I was always depleted of energy, it became very difficult to meet responsibilities at work. In addition, when work became too difficult to manage along with the OCD, I had to quit. I was perceived by family and friends as being lazy, irresponsible, and juvenile. I was always extremely hurt when I was accused of having these qualities. It also hurt to not have anyone understand just what it was that I was going through.
> —Dieter, age thirty-nine

YOU GOTTA SEE THIS!

The television series *Monk* features a character with OCD. Adrian Monk is a retired detective who helps solve crimes. His OCD is in the form of counting objects, issues with contamination, repeating (he brushes his teeth forty times), and arranging objects. His compulsions are addressed in a lighthearted way in this comedy/mystery show.

signs of OCD. You may not be working to your full potential if you're spending time performing rituals unrelated to your work. Maybe you have even quit a job or not applied for a job because of your OCD.

Other related problems include being late to work, not getting enough sleep, and not performing to the best of your ability. These were discussed in the section on school, and the effects are the same in your work life.

Regardless of the type of OCD you have, you can find a job that is right for you. Talk to a mental health professional about what jobs are best suited to your skills and interests.

Just like schools, businesses are required to follow laws that allow people with disabilities the opportunity to work. The Americans with Disabilities Act (ADA) is a federal law that ensures the rights of people with mental or physical disabilities in the workplace. For more information, call 1–800–ADA–WORK or go to http://ada.gov.

WHAT IS OCD? A GUIDE FOR TEACHERS

OCD is an anxiety disorder in which chemicals in the brain cause people to have unwanted, anxiety-provoking thoughts, called obsessions. People with OCD also feel compelled to perform actions, called compulsions, that alleviate the anxiety. They don't want to do this, but they feel anxiety if they don't.

Some common obsessions people with OCD have to deal with are contamination; that they left something on, such as faucets or appliances; and that someone will get hurt if they don't perform a particular action.

In order to relieve the anxiety, people with OCD must carry out a compulsive action. If they feel contaminated, they may wash over and over; if they think they left an appliance on, they may check dozens of times to make sure they turned it off; and if they are trying to avoid hurting someone, they may do a number of actions that are unrelated, such as performing tasks an exact number of times, making sure objects are arranged symmetrically, and so on.

OCD can be hard for students to deal with. It can affect performance on tests and keep them from turning in homework on time, or at all. If you have a student with OCD, it is a good idea to talk with the student about how you can help him or her. The student may need to leave the room occasionally to relax. Sometimes it helps to allow the student more time on tests or have someone in the class take notes for him or her. The two of you might want to meet with the school counselor or psychologist to come up with a plan that works for the student.

NOTES

1. Tamar E. Chansky, *Freeing Your Child from Obsessive-Compulsive Disorder* (New York: Crown, 2000), 316–20.

2. Ibid., 313–14.

3. University of British Columbia, "Obsessive Compulsive Disorder (OCD) Backgrounder," www.publicaffairs.ubc.ca/media/releases/2003/mr-03–08b.html (accessed October 2, 2007).

4. Karen Cassiday, clinical psychologist and a founding fellow in the Academy of Cognitive Therapy, written correspondence with the author, January 2, 2008.

7

Effects of OCD at Home and with Friends

A PERSONAL STORY
John, age nineteen

I am definitely more able to deal with the OCD because I have a stronger support system back home. At school I was on the phone with my parents every day when the OCD got bad and I would also talk to my psychologist often, but I was not able to really focus on it because I was constantly stressed. At school everything became an OCD reminder, and I felt like I did not have a safe haven where I could unwind. At home I don't have as many stressors—no homework or anything and [I] have not been forced to get a job (although I hope to get one soon) and can sleep late and just feel as though I can relax a whole lot more. So that helps with dealing with my OCD, and I also have people with whom I can discuss my experiences candidly. At school I just describe my feelings as being anxious to my roommate (an OCD thing, by the way, because I don't like to tell my friends I have OCD because when I have done this in the past something bad has happened).

HOME

Although many people with OCD are affected in their personal and public life, some people are able to isolate it so it distresses them only at home. Unfortunately, this can be tough on their families.

As you will read in chapter 9, CBT is a very effective treatment for people with OCD. This treatment helps to get your brain to recognize the difference between an OCD thought and a regular thought.

CBT takes time, patience, and support from caring individuals. If you live with others, you will probably need to share with them that you are working on treating your OCD. You will need your loved ones' help.

If you've had OCD for years, your family may have worked out ways to prevent an episode. For example, you may call home to have your mom check that you turned appliances off or you may have your dad repeat a sentence until it sounds just right to you. Unfortunately, their doing these things might not be a healthy solution. If they have been willing to participate in your compulsions, in order to aid you in your treatment, they may need to begin to refrain from doing that. For instance, they might agree to aid in your compulsions less and less often, or they may stop altogether and help you remember that you do not really need the action done but that it is your OCD telling you to have it done. This may be hard on everyone, but it is important.

For some people, it's easier to keep their obsessions and compulsions hidden at school or on the job, but once they get home their OCD takes full control. You don't think it affects your home life? Maybe you don't mind that you spend two hours in the bathroom getting ready in the morning, but have you thought about how your OCD may affect members of your family? Do others in the house have to share a bathroom with you? Do others in your house need to scrub their hands, too, before you feel comfortable at the dining table? Of course, OCD is not something you choose to have, but it is good to be aware that family members might have had to make personal changes as well to accommodate your compulsions, and that definitely affects your home life.

FAMILY REUNION

You might want to ask other members of your family whether they have OCD, too. You may be surprised that you're not the only one.

Have you had a strained relationship with your siblings? If your OCD began when you and your siblings were younger, there may be some resentment on their part that you have received special attention from your parents. They may feel that you received special treats or got out of doing things because of

Certain habits have become so intertwined within my daily routine, I don't even notice sometimes. For example, when it comes to checking if appliances are off, like the faucet or lights, I will count in a set of four. So if I am checking to see if the faucet is off, I will wave my hand underneath four times. I may repeat that set of four again and again when I'm overtired or stressed, because my OCD can ramp up during these times. But while waving my hand underneath the faucet, I will count aloud, "One, two, three, four." Since my dad also has OCD, we have learned to help one another. If one of us is having a difficult time resisting counting, we say together, "One, two three, four—no more," and that usually helps because it's a different voice besides your own telling you to stop.—Claire, age nineteen

your OCD. You may need family counseling to restore these relationships.

If you have younger siblings, they might not understand what you are going through or that what is happening to you is not your choice. And although eventually you might be able to better control your episodes, you will have OCD all your life. Sometimes siblings also start performing your rituals, either to anger you or to get attention. It might be helpful for them to see a therapist as well.

FRIENDS

Friends are supposed to be there through thick and thin, but is that really true? You might have had some friends who couldn't

BROTHERS AND SISTERS

To help them see the world through your eyes, here are some books for your siblings to read:

- *A Thought Is Just a Thought: A Story of Living with OCD*, by Leslie Talley. For ages four to eight. This book is good for young ones also experiencing OCD. Jenny experiences thoughts that if she doesn't perform particular actions, harm will come to her family or her dog. Her thoughts cause her to do things like flip light switches and arrange her crayons in a particular way. She calls these actions "playing the game." The book helps young children understand OCD and how to conquer it with ERP, and explains how it can run in families.

- *Up and Down the Worry Hill*, by Aureen Pinto Wagner, PhD For ages five to nine. This book tells the story of Casey, a boy who repeats, checks, and cleans. He sees a child psychologist who helps him conquer his compulsions through ERP. This book is more suited to younger children who have OCD themselves.

- *Mr. Worry: A Story about OCD*, by Holly Niner. For ages five to ten. This book has information at the front of the book for parents and teachers about OCD. It tells a story about a boy who has compulsions to check. After talking with his parents, he sees a specialist who helps him practice CBT.

- *Multiple Choice*, by Janet Tashjian. For teens. In this fictional account of OCD, the main character, Monica, uses scrabble tiles (A through D) to help her make decisions. Tile A has to be a normal choice, B is a dumb choice, C is a mean choice, and D is a charitable choice. Whichever tile she picks from the bag, she must do. Her "game" ends up with some serious consequences. Although she doesn't want to play, she feels she has to.

- *Kissing Doorknobs*, by Terry Spencer Hesser. For preteens and teens. This fictional story is about an eleven-year-old girl, Tara, who has repeating thoughts and has compulsions to count steps and pray. Because she doesn't want her friends to know of her "habits," she begins to push them away. Her mother has a hard time understanding why Tara has these compulsions, and although she seeks professional help, Tara is not properly diagnosed. It is a good account of how it affects the whole family, as well as friendships. Warning: This book contains some curse words and a sexual assault.

- *Not as Crazy as I Seem*, by George Harrar. For middle school or high school students. A fictional story of a boy whose OCD rituals begin after his grandfather passes away, this book shares his experiences in a new high school and rebellious behavior with a therapist.

- *The Boy Who Couldn't Stop Washing*, by Judith Rapoport. For high school students and adults. A book that came out before many people even knew what OCD was. Shares real accounts of people with OCD.

- *Everything in Its Place: My Trials and Triumphs with Obsessive Compulsive Disorder*, by Marc Summers. For high school students and adults. An autobiography by host of Nickelodeon's *Double Dare* about facing OCD.

A PERSONAL STORY
Dieter, age thirty-nine

Prior to being diagnosed, having OCD completely ruined my home life and my relationship with my family at the time. First of all, since all of my energy was consumed with avoiding things in order not to be contaminated, my tolerance level for things that bothered me was nonexistent. I was always irritable, exhausted, and extremely hurt that no one understood me. In other words, I felt extraordinarily alienated. My only sanctuary was my bedroom, because I only allowed myself and a select few to enter into my space. I didn't even allow the cleaning lady to enter my room. However, problems did occur. For example, if I felt something was contaminated (e.g., a hat, letter, CD, etc.), I would find a place to hide it that was outside of my room. When I was ready to deal with it, I would go back and get it. This could sometimes take months. Well, living with a father that had an obsessive/compulsive personality did not allow for any tolerance of leaving things lying around, even if they were hidden out of the way. If they weren't where they belonged, then they had to be put back in their proper place! As a result, oftentimes I would come home and find a "contaminated" item lying right on my bed or sitting in the middle of my desk. The extreme distress, anxiety, and fear brought on by this discovery usually sent me over the edge and into a rage. It felt like my blood ran cold and surged to my face and head. After a moment, that cold feeling would turn hot, and I would be overcome with the need to find another sanctuary. My father, of course, was the one that usually put these items back in my room. It felt like he was almost putting them there out of spite. I would yell, "Those are my things and this is my room! How dare you touch them without consulting me first! How dare you!" No one knew that the real reason behind my rage was that I was afraid I was going to be infected with HIV if I touched any of those things. It didn't matter that they touched them. "Maybe they, too, would be infected," I thought.

It wasn't until I was diagnosed with OCD that my relationship with my family changed. Prior to being diagnosed I would hear my father yell at me, "You're SICK! You're SICK! Get out of this house before I call the police!" One of my brothers would say to me, "Your behavior is killing Mom. She's gonna die because of you!" Prior to my diagnosis, my mother couldn't understand either, and eventually I was banned from coming into the house.

understand your OCD, especially if it started when you were very young.

Maybe you were the one who ended the friendship out of embarrassment. It can be hard to keep people close when you have a secret you are trying to hide. Some people with OCD have actually avoided making friends through the years. As a result, they may have trouble with friendships. This is something a good therapist can help to work on.

You might want to think about sharing information about your OCD with a few select friends. Choose a friend you know will be understanding and will keep the information

My dad is also a counter, but I don't think he counts every time in even numbers. Both my mom and brother do not have OCD. I know my mom has some knowledge about OCD through books, but I think to my brother OCD is still a mystery. He just doesn't understand why my dad and I have certain habits, but he doesn't treat us like we're crazy. I just think he doesn't know how to help when either of us is struggling. My mom is really my source of guidance when I'm struggling. If I'm able to talk through my feelings and frustrations with her, then I can get a clearer picture on how to lessen my OCD. Since my mom and brother know we have OCD, the topic about the disease has never been tense. Rather, my family has created an atmosphere where I can joke around that I have OCD. In my opinion, laughter is the best medicine. When I say, "Well, there goes my OCD again," it's not a way of degrading myself, but rather saying, "I have OCD. So how am I going to take control so my worries, counting, and thoughts don't take the steering wheel?" Having OCD is part of my life, but accepting that I have OCD is half the battle.—Claire, age nineteen

confidential. Having social supports will be especially helpful if you decide to try behavior therapy, for which you'll need the help of others.

Be aware that by telling others, you may open yourself up to doing activities that trigger your OCD. For instance, you might have avoided going on a vacation with a friend because you would've had to share a hotel room and your friend might find out about your nightly rituals of showering for long periods of time, praying until you get it "just right," brushing and rebrushing your teeth, or washing all objects that came in contact with other people (such as money, credit cards, and pens). Hanging around with others more often means there is a greater chance they will witness some of your obsessive-compulsive behaviors.

Good friends who understand your situation can be helpful for dealing with your OCD. Photo courtesy of istockphoto.com/Sean Locke.

PEOPLE JUST DON'T GET IT

Have you ever tried to tell someone how you have OCD, only to hear them say something like, "So do I! I always have to wash my hands after I take out the garbage." This can be frustrating if your OCD actually runs your life. They mention these small incidents in an attempt to relate to you, but they may not realize the extent to which your OCD impacts your life. What should you do in this situation? According to Dr. Karen Cassiday, clinical psychologist and a founding fellow in the Academy of Cognitive Therapy, some of her patients explain that what they experience is "turbo-charged" compared to what other people experience. It might also help the person understand the difference if you're willing to share specific examples of what you do or the amount of time you spend on your compulsions.

> Prior to being diagnosed, having a social life was very difficult. In many cases it ruined relationships I had with friends. Part of the reason for that was because I avoided interacting with most people because often they would do things that triggered an episode (e.g., want to share food). Also, I was so enveloped in watching, literally, every step I took to make sure I didn't come in contact with something that would contaminate me, that I couldn't be present and enjoy the time I was sharing. Moreover, I was always in the midst of an episode, which made it difficult for me to want to interact with others.—Dieter, age thirty-nine

Some of your friends may have never heard of the disorder or might not understand how severe the disorder can be. You might want to find a good article, Web site, or book to be ready to share with them. You can find resources that may help you in appendix A.

A PERSONAL STORY
Shana, age twenty-seven

OCD is insidious, and because it's a neurochemical disorder in the control center of our bodies, it has free rein to affect normal life activities and function if it's not resisted. For me, one area of impingement is relationships with the other half of my species. It's uncomfortable to write about, but I wanted to challenge myself to go outside my comfort zone. I also wanted to investigate my "self" in more depth with regard to this issue. How has OCD affected my relationships with the opposite sex? I haven't been able to have a relationship. That's right—twenty-seven and never been kissed, as they say. It's difficult to go back home due to the fact that pretty much everyone that I still keep in some contact with [is] married, and many have children. I think there are many ways OCD affects me in this area that I'm not aware of or don't understand yet, and that's on top of fears any girl without OCD has with dating. Now, in addition to OCD, of course, there might be other psychological factors, belief systems, or brain wiring that contributes to my present state.

I remember in high school that if I heard through the grapevine that a certain guy had a crush on me, or I suspected that a guy had designs on me, I would immediately be flooded with a wave of anxiety and would subsequently avoid him or play dumb. But then again, I also remember that the few certain guys who did have a thing for me, I was not attracted to physically, and were not the boys that I would have wanted to be interested in me. Along those lines, there's something to be said about trying to discover how much OCD has to do with my pickiness in men and the very specific type that I find attractive. Nonetheless, when I was informed or became aware of admirers, I felt panicked, I wouldn't know what to do, and I would just be evasive. During this time, OCD was still fairly anonymous and I didn't really grasp the implications of having the disorder. I was not in therapy, and wasn't very educated on the topic. Just hearing about someone liking me would make me anxious, but, as we know, there had to be associated thoughts that came before I'm sure—it's just that when you're drowning in the emotion of fear, especially fear you don't understand, it's difficult to uncover the thoughts underneath. I believe it had something to do with the unknown, something that was scary and had I no experience in, and fear can cause avoidance. And we all know that anxiety can paralyze progress. My mind would jump to lots of conclusions and I would be overwhelmed. Sometimes I would feel that my space was being invaded; I would feel upset and wanted to be left alone—but I think that was a protective mechanism due to the apprehension. The experience would seem like a mixture of our fight or flight response.

Then, and even now, I don't understand, and don't really know how to advance a relationship with a boy who's a friend, to a boyfriend. Mom says she thinks it's because I didn't and still don't know how to flirt. But I say I think I do (isn't that instinct in girls?); I just become extremely self-conscious in that position, "watching" myself, anxious, uncomfortable, and almost feel stupid—so that I try and remove myself from the situation. The thing is, there's no way for me to know if what I feel is any more extreme than someone without OCD, but OCD's got to have something to do with it since I've never really dated for any length of time.

(continued)

In middle and high school, I also remember not being concerned with, or sometimes even interested in, being attached. I was in my mind a lot. It's curious, but I always felt like an outside observer of other people in my peer group, if that makes any sense, or just in a different mind-set altogether. I spent a lot of time with my teachers, not because I wanted to be teacher's pet, but because I seemed to relate better to them and I was attracted to their knowledge. I was a "floater" in school; I didn't belong in a particular group of friends, just knew a lot of different people. I longed to be part of the popular, pretty pack, but that never really worked out. The guys who I thought were cute then (you should see them now) and dated those girls showed no interest even in talking to me. I remember enjoying the energy of high school dances, but never being asked to dance— and that was quite painful, because something in me did long to be noticed.

While some of the girls I knew had been asked as sophomores, juniors, and seniors to prom, I had to ask my prom date to the senior prom. But to me, he happened to be the most handsome guy in the senior class and I couldn't have asked for a more memorable time. I remember when he brought me home; he got out of the car with me to walk me up to the porch, although we didn't get that far. I was so nervous, self-aware, and I kept thinking that I didn't want him to feel like he had to kiss me or something just because he went to the prom with me; I didn't want him to feel obligated. I was analyzing the situation: "Did he get out of the car just because that's the kind of gentlemen he is?"— "What should I say to him?"—"I need to make him feel that he shouldn't have to do anything he thinks he should"—"He's too wonderful and handsome; I'm not in his league." Yes, I wanted him to be interested in me, and I wanted to know what beginning something I hadn't known before would be like, but the next thing I know my parents are driving down the street and into the driveway, and we uneventfully parted ways. Writing about it now, I wish I could go back to that moment and see what would have happened had my parents not pulled in the driveway.

At present, I would like to attempt to push myself, just like this narrative, beyond my comfort zone. I'm on the lookout for places where I might meet a guy that shares my affinities and just think of it as an experience, not that I need to look for someone to date, because that will create anxiety. One thing that haunts me is how to tell that someone that I struggle with OCD; I mean it affects me every day of my life—I sometimes think of it as baggage I didn't make the choice to carry on my journey in life. But as my mother always says, "Everyone has something, even though they may seem put together."

WHAT IS OCD? A GUIDE FOR FRIENDS

OCD is an anxiety disorder in which chemicals in the brain cause people to have unwanted anxiety-provoking thoughts, called obsessions. People with OCD also feel compelled to perform actions, called compulsions, that alleviate the anxiety. The person doesn't want to do this but feels anxiety if he or she doesn't perform these actions.

Some common obsessions people with OCD have dealt with are contamination; that they left something on, such as faucets or appliances; or that someone will get hurt if they don't perform a particular action.

In order to relieve the anxiety, people with OCD must carry out compulsive actions. If they feel contaminated, they may wash over and over; if they think they left an appliance on, they may check dozens of times to make sure they turned it off; and if they are trying to avoid hurting someone, they may perform actions that are unrelated, such as performing tasks an exact number of times, making sure objects are arranged symmetrically, and so on.

Having OCD can be hard for people to deal with, and sometimes they don't want to talk about it. Being a good friend means you are understanding about this. It might be helpful to just let your friend know you are there if she or he wants to talk about it. From time to time your friend may want you to help her or him think about something else to get her or his mind off the obsession.

8 Getting Help from Mental Health Professionals

A PERSONAL STORY
John, age nineteen

I have basically compiled a master OCD list and on this list I have written everything that is related to my OCD. So today I went to see my psychologist and he said from 12:00–1:00 and 4:00–5:00 p.m., devote an hour knocking down rituals on this list. Focusing on songs that I can't listen to or movies that I never watched— things like that. Or placing the remote in a different spot rather than the designated OCD "spot" in my room.

With me, the reason I feel this will be a success is I am more dedicated to the program. In the past I felt like I had something to lose. I can compare it to a diet; it is almost like a person who has been dieting for years on and off but never really wants to abandon the sweets that they love or finds a comfort in food; they feel like they have something to lose. But then one day they go to the doctor who tells them they have to lose weight or they are going to pass away soon. It was like I always had something to lose and I had that eye-opening experience in college where I realized I am going to keep this OCD "weight" on unless I devote myself 100 percent to the diet. And when I say 100 percent, it is not like I am completely immersed in CBT [cognitive behavioral therapy]; it is more I am taking small steps each day and slowly implementing the strategies into my life.

WHOM SHOULD I SEE?

If you think you may have OCD, it is a good idea to get a professional opinion. One place to start is to go to your primary care doctor; he or she can help you find the right mental health professional for you.

Some therapists' offices are so cozy that they could double as a person's living room. Photo courtesy of Melanie Justice.

The four most common types of mental health professionals are the following:

- ◎ *Therapist:* This title is often used when describing any mental health professional; it is a generic term that includes social workers, counselors, psychologists, psychiatrists, and psychoanalysts.

- ◎ *Psychologist:* A mental health professional with a PhD or PsyD in psychology. He or she is not able to prescribe medication, except in some states and in the military.

- ◎ *Psychoanalyst:* A kind of psychologist who concentrates on the subconscious thoughts (Sigmund Freud was the pioneer of this branch of psychology); not commonly used for OCD (it is a subcategory of a type of therapist).

- ◎ *Psychiatrist:* A physician who prescribes medication for mental health disorders.

To make things simpler, the word "therapist" is used to refer to therapists and psychologists throughout this book.

If you need both behavioral therapy and medication to control your OCD, you may end up seeing both a therapist (for treatment) and a psychiatrist (for medication).

When choosing a professional to begin working with, you will want to ask about that professional's experience in working with OCD. You will also want to know if he or she is familiar with (cognitive behavioral therapy (CBT) and exposure with response prevention (ERP) (see chapter 9 for more information about these treatments). If the professional isn't that familiar with CBT or ERP, you may want to keep looking. If you go to the OCF Web site at www.ocfoundation.org and click on the link "Treatment Providers List—Online," you may be able to find someone in your area.

The root *psych* means "mind."

Once you choose a mental health professional, you will want to be honest with him or her and share as much about your obsessions and compulsions as you can. You may want to give your relationship with your therapist a couple of sessions before you decide whether it is a good match for you. Remember that you are not looking for someone who is nice but for someone who can help you overcome your anxiety and OCD—your mental health professional is going to make you work. You probably will get homework—exercises to try at home. Will he or she know if you actually did them? No, but realize that if you decide not to complete them, you aren't helping your treatment process.

One concern some people have that prevents them from seeking medical help is confidentiality. They are afraid the information they tell their therapist will be shared with others (including their parents, if they are under the age of eighteen). By law, therapists cannot share your file with anyone unless you confess intentions to hurt yourself or others, if they believe a child is in danger, or if you are involved in a court case and the information is subpoenaed by a judge. (There may be added limitations for your particular state; you can always find out the laws before beginning treatment.) Your therapist will discuss with you when and how to share information with your family.

ERP BY PHONE

Not everyone lives near an adequate mental health professional. Maybe you found a good one but you moved or are in college. With modern technology, you can still be a patient of a good mental health professional. Psychiatrists have been able to check up on patients by phone for years. They sometimes do this just to make sure the dosage of medicine is correct and may only need to have a conversation that can be accomplished by phone.

Now, some therapists are also open to the option of regular telephone appointments. There are some benefits talking to a therapist from home instead of at the office. As already mentioned, phone appointments work for people who

YOU GOTTA READ THIS!

***Rewind, Replay, Repeat: A Memoir of Obsessive-Compulsive Disorder*, by Jeff Bell**

Radio newsman Jeff Bell begins his autobiography with what he refers to as the "normal years." Sound familiar to you? Although he had one recurring OCD situation as a child, it stopped, giving him a "normal" childhood and teenage life. He then gives detail after excruciating detail of his ordeal with OCD as an adult: he was a victim of unwanted and ruminating (obsessively repeating) thoughts. These obsessive thoughts went on for a long period of time, and he could not let them go. They were mostly of doing harm to others if he didn't pick up objects on the ground and along the highway. Bell shares his experiences with therapy, CBT, medication, and finally seeing the light.

A PERSONAL STORY
Ainsley, age fifteen

My first ever meeting with an OCD therapist occurred in the year of 2006 when I was about fourteen. I remember when the doctor walked through the door to the waiting room and called my name. It was then that I looked around the waiting room, hoping that there might just be another patient with my same name that the appointment was meant for.

There wasn't.

I began to follow her back into her little therapy room. Therapists' offices, as I've learned, are either extremely well lit or as dim as my grandmother's house. Dim meaning all the lights are turned off, but for a few porcelain lamps strategically placed about the room with an orangey-peachy lampshade giving off an eerily warm glow. Hers had a large window, and the lights were all on. She was a well-lit therapist.

She began asking the typical questions. I'd met with plenty other therapists before, just not for the purpose of OCD medication. And so I answered her questions. Though something alarmed me. I was completely calm and I was having . . . could it be . . . fun? Yes. I was actually enjoying answering these questions and telling her every little thing about my life. Here she was, just nodding along and taking notes. I was a goddess! Whatever I said was simply written down and given a nod of approval. I was tempted to let myself get a bit carried away. "Well let's see, Doctor Whatsyourface . . . I've been experimented upon by aliens twelve times since last June, I am so tough that I literally eat nails for breakfast, and I'm the spawn of Satan."

But I didn't. I told the truth, like a good little girl, and answered her questions. She put me on medicine, of which [kind] I can't remember, and that was that.

do not live close to an appropriate therapist. If that's the case for you, by having phone conversations, you can still "meet" regularly with your therapist. The main benefit is that you can have your therapist "there with you" as you complete your therapy homework, whether it's at your home or at your work. Many people have obsessions and compulsions that occur only in certain environments that can't be simulated at their therapist's office.

Maybe your therapist is having you work on performing your ritual only once instead of over and over. This will naturally cause you anxiety. But if you have your therapist on the phone, he or she can talk you through those first fifteen minutes when you want to give in to your OCD. You can also report to the therapist your level of anxiety as you work through the situation.

This is also helpful because phone ERP can be done before or after regular office hours. You may also be able to have your appointment before school or work, when your OCD may be flaring up.

Phone ERP may be less expensive than in-person appointments for two reasons: You are not at the office, where the therapist has to cover the costs of a receptionist and building utilities in his or her fees, and the phone call is usually shorter than a full therapy session would be.

Usually phone ERP is a scheduled appointment during which you perform your ERP homework while being coached by your therapist. Sometimes your therapist will allow you to call when you are having a meltdown so that he or she can try to walk you through conquering it. You should remember, however, that this is not always an option because your therapist may have appointments with other patients.

Before you begin phone ERP, you may need to attend a few regular office visits to get to know your therapist. The therapist might want to see your house so that he or she can better envision your situation. Phone ERP is more effective with particular types of OCD than with others. Your therapist can explain which types you have that might apply to phone ERP. In addition, some forms of OCD are not at all conducive to phone ERP—for instance, it is not safe to be performing ERP on your cell phone while driving, so it would not work if your OCD occurs when you drive.[1]

If you would like to try phone ERP, you will want to find out whether insurance covers it. The therapist may charge you only a partial fee instead of a fee for a full session, but it is something you want to look into before you begin.

A TALK WITH A THERAPIST: WHAT TO EXPECT

Are you a little nervous about seeing a therapist for the first time? It might help to know what will happen in the first couple sessions. Here is what psychotherapist Melanie Justice does when she first meets with a new client:

The first session, sometimes called an initial evaluation, assessment, or intake, is usually spent gathering information and getting to know you and your background. Some of the questions a therapist might ask in the first session include "How long have you had your OCD symptoms and how are they affecting your daily life?" and "What are the thoughts or images that go through your mind before you engage in a ritual?" The therapist might also ask something general, such as what your relationship with your parents is like. It is important to provide answers that are as honest and complete as possible so that your therapist can understand your situation and can help you more effectively. It's also a good idea to come to the first session prepared with any questions you might have, either about therapy, your OCD, or the therapist's background and experience with anxiety disorders.

Usually during either the first or the second session, the therapist might give you an assessment called the Y-BOCS (Yale-Brown Obsessive-Compulsive Scale) or the CY-BOCS (Children's Yale-Brown Obsessive-Compulsive Scale) if you are under eighteen; he or she will ask a series of questions about your obsessions and compulsions and how frequently they occur. For example, you might say that you have an obsession involving fear of blurting out insults or obscenities and a compulsion such as excessive hand washing, and that you engage in each of these approximately four hours per day.

After the first session, the content of the remainder of the sessions will vary, depending on the thoroughness of your therapist's assessment of you, the amount of pscyhoeducation he or she provides you, and how motivated you are to start treatment. Your therapist might ask you to purchase an OCD treatment manual or workbook that has exercises and information in it that you will use in conjunction with therapy, so sometimes the session material will be dependent on how the workbook is structured.

Typically, a therapist would probably continue your evaluation in the second session, until he or she is sure he or she has enough information to develop a treatment plan tailored just for you. During one of the first three or four sessions, your therapist will probably give you psychoeducation about the nature of anxiety in general and, more specifically, about OCD. He or she will then explain the most effective treatment for OCD, which is ERP. If there's anything you don't understand about ERP, ask your therapist for more information or examples of how and why it works. He or she should be very patient and understanding that what you are going through is very difficult and that treatment will probably sound overwhelming at first.

During the fourth or fifth session, you and your therapist may start working on designing a treatment plan together. The two of you will create a fear hierarchy by brainstorming what kinds of exposures might cause you to become anxious, such as touching a public doorknob if you have a fear of contamination, or by messing up a neat stack of books if you have obsessions about symmetry, for instance. You [will] then rank the different exposures in order, from least to most scary. Your therapist will talk to you about the importance of just sitting with your anxiety when doing exposures, and may give you some helpful tips. You aren't allowed to ritualize [perform your compulsive actions or thoughts] after doing an exposure, so your therapist should help you understand why this is so important.

Typically [at some point] after the fifth session, once your fear hierarchy has been established and you feel that you fully understand and agree with the rationale behind ERP, you will start to actually do your exposures. You will start with the least frightening exposures first so that you don't become too overwhelmed. Usually, you will do at least the first exposure with your therapist, and then you will most likely practice at home until it no longer frightens you and you don't have the urge to ritualize anymore.

Depending on the number of sessions you have per week, you will probably conquer about one exposure item on your fear hierarchy per week until you make it all the way to the top of the hierarchy. You may find that you need to tell your therapist to move some items on the hierarchy around as you go, because you might discover that you aren't ready for some exposures that you thought you would be at that point. Alternatively, exposures that you originally thought would be very difficult might seem like they might be easy for you now.

The end of your treatment program will involve making sure you have extinguished the rituals and obsessions you targeted at the beginning of treatment, as well as identifying any others that are a problem for you. If there are other behaviors you'd like to work on, let your therapist know that you'd like to continue therapy. If not, you'll learn some strategies to help you if you temporarily relapse. Overall, there is no magic number of sessions you'll need—you can treat mild OCD in as few as twelve sessions, although this is rare, or it can take as long as several months.[2]

NOTE

1. William M. Gordon, "Doing Exposure/Response Prevention with the Cell Phone" (lecture, Obsessive-Compulsive Foundation National Conference, Atlanta, GA, July 22, 2006).

2. Melanie Justice, psychotherapist, written correspondence with the author, December 10, 2006.

Getting Help through Cognitive Behavioral Therapy

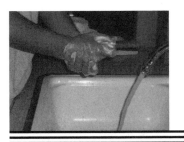

Therapy can sound overwhelming. You just need to take it step by step. Photo courtesy of istockphoto.com/ Rey Rojo.

WHAT IS CBT?

A commonly used technique for treating OCD is cognitive behavioral therapy (CBT), also referred to as cognitive behavior therapy. This form of therapy is conducted by a professional, and it involves implementing strategies for fighting OCD at home and in your daily life. CBT requires a lot of work from you and your family. In order for it to be successful, you need to be committed and patient. Just think of the results, though: being able to conquer your unwanted thoughts and actions.

The word *cognitive* means "related to thinking." In the case of cognitive therapy, you become consciously aware of your thoughts and work on changing that thinking. You learn to recognize your OCD thoughts, and you work on acknowledging them as OCD thoughts and resisting the urge to ritualize in response to them. The word *behavior* refers to the actions (usually rituals) that happen as a result of your compulsions.

For instance, if you worry about leaving the stove on when you leave your house, you might work on recognizing those thoughts as OCD "false alarms" (cognitive) and also on resisting the urge to return to the house to make sure the stove is off (behavior).

The main goal of CBT is to be able to overcome your compulsions and, by doing so, reduce the frequency of obsessive thoughts. You are trying to identify when a thought is an OCD thought and then not react to it—in other words, to resist performing your compulsion.

WHAT HAPPENS TO YOUR BRAIN WHEN YOU RECEIVE CBT

As discussed in chapter 4, when you have OCD, parts of your brain such as the orbital frontal cortex and the basal ganglia are overactive. What both CBT and certain medications do is to help those parts of your brain work the way they should.

Using CBT, you will begin to recognize when a thought is real versus when it is an OCD thought. This is something that

PAVLOV'S DOG, LITTLE ALBERT, AND A BUNCH OF RATS

Ivan Pavlov didn't start out in the field of psychology, but he conducted one of the most well-known experiments in psychology (and had one of the most famous dogs of psychology salivating at his results). Pavlov, a physiologist from Russia, won a Nobel Prize in 1904 for his work on digestion, which was the starting point for his psychological experiment.

Pavlov was conducting experiments on salivary secretions as a result of altered conditions with foods. He used his dog as the subject. When Pavlov's assistant brought food to the dog, not surprisingly, the dog began to salivate before he even ate it. Pavlov was fascinated.

In the 1900s Pavlov pursued experiments to see if the brain could make this connection between the food and some other stimulus. He rang a bell and then put food in the dog's mouth. Soon the dog began salivating at the sound of the bell alone, even when food wasn't present. This is what's now referred to as classical, or Pavlovian, conditioning. A stimulus such as the bell, which normally would not cause a physiological or reflex reaction (referred to as a conditioned stimulus), is paired with something that would normally cause such a reaction (referred to as the unconditioned stimulus), such as the food. After these are paired, the response that would have occurred only with the unconditioned stimulus now occurs with the conditioned stimulus as well.

In the late 1910s John Watson performed a new set of experiments on a boy referred to as "Little Albert." The poor eleven-month-old was subjected to loud noises as he reached to pet a white rat. Not surprisingly, Little Albert became frightened, relating the noise to the rat. What was significant is that he also became frightened of other objects that were white, even Watson wearing a white Santa beard.

In the 1920s and 1930s another scientist, B. F. Skinner, created more studies pairing a conditioned and unconditioned stimulus. Instead of pairing something like a bell with a physiological or reflex reaction (like salivating or fear), he paired a behavior with a reward. First he used rats as his subjects. When a rat pressed down on a bar, a pellet of food would drop into a feeding bowl. With time, the rats learned that there was a relationship between pressing the bar and receiving food. This type of conditioning is called operant conditioning. People use operant conditioning all the time to shape human and animal behavior. Training your dog with a treat would be an example; another example is when teachers put stickers and smiley faces on their students' papers when they've done well.

As you might assume, this discovery can be applied to many aspects of people's lives. But the pairings between the unconditioned stimulus with the conditioned stimulus is not always beneficial. For instance, if your alarm clock were to begin ringing right now, you might feel a moment of dread, since the sound of it is usually paired with being awakened involuntarily from sleep. (This would be classical conditioning.)

Now imagine a guy who has obsessions about contamination and compulsions to wash. When he feels he is contaminated with germs, he experiences anxiety. When he washes, he gets rid of that anxiety. He is learning that washing rids him of anxiety—not a very functional pairing because it leads to more and more compulsive behavior. In this chapter, we will discuss how CBT can help to change your compulsive behaviors.

family and friends can help you to recognize. They may even have to remind you of this when you begin your CBT. For example, at first it might take others to help you recognize that you are tapping the light switch seven times. After a while, you're able to notice this yourself and realize it's your OCD making you do this: Nothing bad will happen if you refrain from doing it.

Part of CBT is overcoming your compulsions. Your therapist will make you face your anxiety instead of suppressing it or finding ways to distract yourself when it occurs. He or she will want you to work through your feelings of anxiety as you avoid performing your compulsive behavior.

It is important to keep a journal of your CBT. Whenever you are attempting to resist an OCD urge, write down the following:

- time;
- date;
- intensity of the urge;
- what might have triggered the incident; and
- how long you were able to resist the urge to carry out your compulsive behavior.

Over time, you may begin to know when a thought is just your OCD talking and be able to ignore it with minimal anxiety.

ERP

It's time to get our hands dirty—literally, for some. A common CBT treatment used for OCD is ERP therapy. During ERP, you are asked to confront a compulsion you experience. Your therapist will start small and slowly raise the bar on what you will be asked to do. For example, people with a fear of contamination might be asked to imagine their hands touching a toilet. Then they may be asked to actually touch the handle of a toilet. Next, they may have to touch the seat of the toilet. Eventually, they may even have to touch the inside of the toilet.

This may sound extreme. After all, how often do people put their hands in a toilet in regular life? So why would a professional have a person who fears germs do that? Part of the ERP is to heighten a person's anxiety so that over time, the person's body acts less severely to the stimulus. This is called habituation. Imagine hearing a loud sound, smelling a bad smell, or swimming in cold water. After you experience one of these for a while, you get used to it and are less bothered. The same happens with your anxiety. In treatment, you might be asked to imagine touching the bottom of your shoe and not getting a chance to wash your hands. The first time you hear this, you may have a high level of anxiety, but after hearing this scenario day after day, you will be less bothered by the thought, and maybe even bored with hearing it.

When people with OCD find that no harm comes to them from an exposure that seems extreme, they are more likely to be able to touch everyday objects they used to avoid, such as money or doorknobs.

Some obsessions and compulsions require more imagery than actual actions. If you have a fear that you might leave the lights on in your house when you leave and a whole chain of events will happen, you can try out that scenario, and you will find nothing happens. However, if you fear leaving the stove on, it is not a good idea to turn the stove on and leave the house— something *could* happen! So you can't actually play the scenario out in reality. Instead, your therapist might have you imagine you left it on. Then he or she may run a whole scenario through your mind of all the awful things that can happen because of this. The therapist may have you brainstorm what will happen; this is called imaginal exposure. If you do this day after day, you get tired of it and it starts to sound silly. Your anxiety lessens. (You can read more about this later in this chapter, in the section titled "Imaginal Exposure.")

Therapists may also ask you to create an area in your home that is designated as "OCD-free." This is an area in your house where you cannot perform your compulsive behaviors. Maybe it's at the dinner table, where you eat your peas in pairs, or in

A PERSONAL STORY
Dieter, age thirty-nine

Cognitive behavior therapy has been an essential part of my recovery. In short, it showed me that many times the anticipatory anxiety that I felt prior to doing an exposure was oftentimes much worse than the actual anxiety I felt when actually doing the exposure. Also, most times I did my first exposure in the office during a session with my therapist. Having my therapist guide, instruct, and observe is extremely helpful. For instance, the therapist is able to model for me how to go about doing the exposure on my own. In addition, if the exposure is incredibly difficult for me to begin on my own, the therapist is able to provide the necessary encouragement that will get me started.

I have now been able to incorporate cognitive behavior therapy into my daily life. Instead of avoiding something, I have the skills to expose myself to something that I would otherwise avoid. Therefore, instead of having an episode and doing the CBT later, I can skillfully address a spontaneous situation by first acknowledging that the anxiety will dissipate, and, secondly, being mindful that any anticipatory anxiety I may have will likely be less than the actual anxiety I feel once the exposure begins.

the family room, where you ask your family members to repeat the lines said on television until they sound "just right" to you. By doing this, you are overpowering your OCD, telling it, "You can't get to me here." Imagine how relieving it would be to keep OCD from invading your entire life!

HABITUATION

Imagine riding a roller coaster one hundred times in a row. The first time you ride it, you might feel petrified and experience anxiety. As you continue to ride it, each drop and loop may scare you a little less. Eventually, you may not feel scared or anxious at all. The same can be true when treating OCD with ERP therapy. When you are going through ERP, your anxiety will peak before it drops. As your therapist gives you a situation to imagine or to try out, you will feel uncomfortable at first. As you get more used to the situation, you begin to adjust.

A PERSONAL STORY
Claire, age nineteen

I use the phrase "difficult time resisting counting" [for what affects me] because you become so convinced that certain appliances are not off that you continue to check and recheck. Even if I finally manage to walk away from the source, I can get this urge to go back and double-check if it's off. So I have to preoccupy my brain with something completely different.

Since I was eight years old, I have been going to a psychologist to talk about my challenges with OCD and preplan tricks to prevent the counting from getting the best of me. Those tricks may include playing the piano, walking my dogs, going to the gym, or watching a movie. If I can stimulate my brain with another activity, then I will forget about that urge to count.

IMAGINAL EXPOSURE

Sometimes it's not just one component of your OCD that needs you to imagine a situation versus actually performing it—it is the entire form of your OCD, such as unwanted thoughts. These can be things such as worrying that you've run over people in your car, fearing you'll stab someone in your sleep, or fearing you'll open the emergency exit on a plane.

Because of this, therapists will sometimes use imaginal exposure. As with ERP in real or actual situations, your therapist will first help you create a list of actions and thoughts

YOU GOTTA READ THIS!

Talking Back to OCD: The Program That Helps Kids and Teens Say "No Way"—and Parents Say "Way to Go," by John S. March

A great resource for the whole family that walks them through CBT, this book has separate sections: one for parents of someone with OCD and one for the teen or child with OCD. It gives the reader an "OCD toolkit," or ways to conquer OCD. It also shares personal stories of kids and teens of all ages and their experiences using CBT.

AUTHOR'S STORY

Did I Leave the Garage Door Open?

I have anxiety when I leave my house and am not sure whether I closed the garage door. I worry about whether my bike is in plain view and will be swiped within five minutes of my leaving. I continue to drive away as I tell myself, "Oh, well—no time to go back." This would be similar to using exposure with response prevention. Usually a couple of streets later, I'm singing along to the radio. By the time I get to work, it's out of my mind. When I get back home, as I press the button to open the garage door, I don't even think about the fact that I was worried earlier. I don't think to check whether my bike is still there.

that bother you. You may then be asked to help put them in order from least to most anxiety provoking. This list might then be turned into a script read to you by your therapist, read by you aloud, or recorded with your voice and played repeatedly on an audiotape. The length of the scripts can vary. Most scripts use as many of your senses as they can to really form an image in your head. Here are examples of such scripts that may

ANIMAL OCD

Can you believe that animals are also thought to have behavior similar to OCD? Dogs can have a condition called canine compulsive disorder (CCD). Some of their compulsive behaviors include tail-chasing, spinning, and licking. It is thought to be aggravated by frustration (such as at being chained up), stress, or boredom.

As with humans, the best treatment for animals seems to be behavior therapy. Family members are told to ignore the compulsive behavior and reward noncompulsive behavior. Medications such as Anafranil and Prozac are sometimes used to help regulate serotonin levels. Families should also make sure that their dogs are getting enough exercise.[1]

Other animals that have shown signs of a similar disorder are cats, which pull out their fur; horses, which bite at their flanks; and birds, which pick at their feathers.[2]

be created for a person who has a fear of running people over with his or her car and has a compulsion to keep checking the route driven and/or watching the news for evidence.

"You are driving along the road you always take to work, when you feel a clunk on the side of your car. You look out your rearview mirror and see a deer scampering away. Your car must have only nicked it because it is running rather quickly into the woods."

"You are driving along the road you always take to work, when you feel a bump under your car. You pull over and get out to find that you've run over a skunk. You call the city to report it, and they say they will send someone out to clean it up."

"You are driving along the road you always take to work, when you feel a bump under your car. You look back to see a child crying on the side of the road. When you get out, you notice he is clutching his foot. You call an ambulance and it takes him to the nearest hospital. It turns out that you ran over his foot when he was running across the street to retrieve a ball. His parents send you the hospital and doctors' bills, and your car insurance goes up."

"You are driving along the road you always take to work, when you hear a thunk under your car. You stop the car and get out to find you've hit a small child. He is unconscious. Another car stops and the driver assists you. Once the ambulance comes, the paramedics are able to bring the child back to consciousness. The man who helped you yells at you for being a careless driver. You break out into a sweat, and the cold air makes you shiver. You receive a ticket for speeding and failing to yield to a pedestrian. The boy's parents also take you to court to pay for the hospital bills as well as mental anguish. You end up needing to take on a second job to help pay for the costs of your lawyer and the amount of the judgment against you."

"You are driving along the road you always take to work, when you hear a thunk as you drive over something. You look back and see a young man lying in the street. You slam on your brakes, squealing your tires. You quickly pull over and call for help. As you get closer, you can see he has suffered a head injury. There is blood on the street, and the man isn't moving. Once the ambulance comes, they pronounce him dead. You are sued by the man's family for the pain and suffering they have endured. You have to see his family's faces, including the man's young children, when you appear in court."

"You are driving along the road you always take to work, when you hear a woman scream and feel your front tires hit something. You slam on the brakes, pull over, and get out of your car. You see a young child lying in the street. You get out your cell phone, your fingers slipping on the keypad. As you call for help, the mother runs toward her child, hysterical. There is a smell of burned rubber and blood. You try to revive the child, who is unconscious, by performing CPR. The ambulance comes and takes the child, along with his mother, to the hospital, where later he is pronounced dead. The mother accuses you of intentionally hitting her child. After a week's trial, you are found guilty of manslaughter. You are taken to prison in handcuffs, where you spend ten years of your life."

Although this treatment style may sound shocking, these are images that might run through someone's head while driving, forcing him or her to backtrack to be sure he or she didn't hit

YOU GOTTA HAVE COURAGE

It's time to rent the movie *The Wizard of Oz*. If you've started CBT, then you definitely have the *brains* to know it may very well work and the *heart* to want to receive help for yourself and your loved ones. Now all you need is *courage*.

Jack Rachman, PhD, a professor at the University of British Columbia, and his colleagues conducted a study interviewing bomb disposal operators to find out their level of fear. Before they began their training, they were 60 percent confident. By the time they had disarmed at least one bomb, their confidence had gone up to around 97 percent.[3] It's amazing that someone can feel confident in disarming a bomb. That really shows the power of ERP treatment.

EXAMPLE OF ERP FOR NTK-OCD

If you remember from chapter 2, one type of OCD, called "NTK-OCD," causes people with it to ask meaningless questions, needing to find out the answers.

As with other forms of OCD, NTK-OCD can be treated with CBT. Allowing time to pass without asking a question or receiving an answer can alleviate the anxiety the person feels. Dr. William Gordon, a licensed psychologist, suggests fighting these urges little by little, one area of questions at a time. For example, if the person's questions are often about television, meals, and school, he or she may want to first try to cut down on asking questions about what's on television, and then work on the other areas.

ERP can also be used to help reduce incidences of NTK-OCD. The person can be exposed to situations in which he or she would want to ask questions but not get the chance to know the answer. Imagine watching a television game show such as *Who Wants to Be a Millionaire?* The million-dollar question has been asked, but the contestant hasn't yet given the answer. Will the contestant know the answer? Will he or she get it right? Part of ERP therapy may be to turn off the TV before you have a chance to find out; you will feel anxiety as this happens, but eventually you learn that the anxiety will lessen. Later, you will find you don't really care what the question or the answer was.[4]

anyone. As the person hears the script over and over, it will become less shocking to him or her, cause less anxiety, and might even appear ridiculous. That is the purpose of imaginal exposure. Sometimes the patient will then write a new script with the therapist to work on a new topic or to expand his or her exposure. For example, someone who has a fear of germs might only be able to imagine not washing his or her hands for a couple of hours as the highest anxiety-producing situation he or she can currently handle; as he or she becomes more comfortable with that scenario, new scripts can be added.

HIERARCHIES

Hierarchies are highly individual and vary greatly from person to person. Your therapist will guide you in creating your hierarchy based on specific situations that make you anxious. You will rate the situations on a scale of 0 to 100, with 0 being "not anxiety provoking at all," and 100 being "most anxiety provoking." Your therapist will probably want you to start with an exposure exercise that you've rated somewhere in the middle, such as a forty or fifty, so that the situation causes you to feel anxious but is not overwhelming.

The ranking depends on each particular person's rating of the events. You may feel that what one person considers low anxiety producing is high on your list, or vice versa. Below are some examples of hierarchies for various types of OCD.

Contamination

1. **LOW ANXIETY: Touch the doorknob at a public place.**
2. **Eat a meal without washing your hands first.**
3. **Sit in the chair of someone you consider "dirty."**
4. **Sit on your bed with "dirty clothes" on.**
5. **Sit on a toilet in a public restroom.**
6. **HIGH ANXIETY: Touch an object that was on the floor of a public restroom.**

Checking

1. **LOW ANXIETY: Leave the house after checking only twice that things are turned off.**
2. **Leave a curling iron or regular iron on and go in another room for ten minutes.**
3. **Turn the faucet on low and let it drip for sixty minutes.**
4. **Leave the front door unlocked and walk around the block.**
5. **Leave an automatic-shutoff curling iron on and leave the house for a short errand.**
6. **HIGH ANXIETY: Leave your computer on and leave the house.**

Fear of Harming Others

1. **LOW ANXIETY: Do imaginal exposure of yourself harming someone.**
2. **Draw a picture of yourself stabbing someone.**

3. Be in the presence of a person you fear harming.

4. Hold a mildly sharp object in your hand when in the presence of a person you fear stabbing.

5. HIGH ANXIETY: Hold a very sharp knife in your hand when in the presence of a person you fear stabbing.

Fear of Homosexuality

1. LOW ANXIETY: Spend at least sixty minutes in a room with a same-sex friend.

2. Sit on a couch with a same-sex friend.

3. Touch a same-sex friend's arm while talking with him or her.

4. HIGH ANXIETY: Do imaginal exposure of having a sexual encounter with a member of the same sex and all the feared consequences related to that—e.g., being found out, being teased or harassed, etc.

Repeating

1. LOW ANXIETY: Say a sentence without repeating it, even if it was "imperfect."

2. Add something only once; do not repeat the calculation.

3. Read the last sentence of a paragraph only once, even if you didn't understand it.

4. Get dressed only once; do not change clothes.

5. HIGH ANXIETY: Do not repeat a sentence in your head, even if you think repeating it will prevent something bad from happening.

Fear of Hitting Someone/Running Someone Over with Your Car

1. LOW ANXIETY: Drive no more than five miles per hour under the speed limit.

2. Drive without someone else in the car to reassure you that you didn't hit anyone.

3. Back out of a parking spot and drive away without checking that you backed into someone.

4. HIGH ANXIETY: Drive one way to your destination and another way home, so that you are unable to check your route.[5]

HOW FAMILY CAN HELP

If you have had OCD for years, chances are your family has made accommodations for you. Their intentions were either to be helpful or to avoid an upsetting situation they didn't want to deal with. Having a family member involved in the checking, cleaning, or other compulsion to help lower your anxiety is not helpful for you in the long run—it's considered enabling. Instead, have that person agree to help you face your anxiety or reduce your stress. He or she could join you in shooting baskets or going for a walk. Be sure he or she knows that this is hard for you and that you might not be able to overtake your OCD every time or for the amount of time you planned.

If you make it to your desired time, treat yourself to something: a movie, a manicure, or something else you enjoy. Be sure it is a healthy reward and not something that will become a bad habit, such as a soft drink or a food reward.

INTENSIVE TREATMENT PROGRAMS

People who are so greatly affected by OCD that they cannot function on their own will need more assistance. These people benefit from intensive treatment programs, either outpatient programs lasting an entire day or inpatient programs that last for weeks or months. These programs can help teach people to face their fears. Some programs can help people with comorbid conditions (disorders that often occur in conjunction with OCD, discussed in more depth in chapter 12), such as Asperger's Disorder, eating disorders, and body dysmorphic disorder (BDD).

If you enter a treatment program, you may be asked to do everyday tasks that help you live a regular life. For example, if you have a fear of contamination so severe that you are unable to leave your house and so aren't attending school, aren't interacting with other people, and are having suicidal thoughts, you might benefit from being in an intensive treatment program. There, you might have to perform tasks that serve as exercises that will help you function in the real world, such as showering for a minimal amount of time or cleaning a bathroom.

A PERSONAL STORY
Michelle, age sixteen

In the spring of my freshman school year, my family, therapists, and I all agreed that I had made little progress in months, despite my outpatient therapy and current medication regime, and that I needed to be completely immersed in treatment, as this would help me get better the fastest. At this time, because of my OCD, I was unable to be with certain people, to be in certain public places, and to use any public bathrooms. I was being home/hospital-based tutored because it was too difficult for me to be in school.

My family and I had heard great things about Menninger, a hospital in Houston, Texas, that had a treatment program for teens with obsessive-compulsive disorder. At the end of May I was admitted to Menninger. As much as I did not want to be away from home for so long, I was actually somewhat excited about going there, as I wanted to get better and have my life back. I was, of course, very nervous, as I knew this was going to be extremely hard work; however, I was ready for the challenge.

I was in treatment for nine and one-half weeks at Menninger, and in that time I saw my OCD getting better and better. The most exciting thing about Menninger was that I was able to meet other teens with OCD, as at home I did not know anyone who had severe symptoms like I did. As supportive as my family, friends, doctor, and therapist had been at home, I found that I could connect with the teens there on a whole other level, as we really knew what the others were going through. We became really close and we all encouraged and motivated each other. There was so much support there, between the wonderful, expert staff and the teens. When I returned from Houston, I was doing so much better; my symptoms had been reduced tremendously and I now carried important coping strategies with me.

A year has now passed since I returned from Menninger, and I am still continuing to do really well. I have not relapsed; however, I recognize that OCD is a lifelong struggle and there most probably will be times in the future when I am struggling again with my OCD. I completed my sophomore year at a new school, and have continued to do CBT therapy on an outpatient basis. I feel much more open about having OCD and am starting a teen support group in my area so that I can try to help others in one of the ways that was so effective for me, being the opportunity to connect with other people with OCD.

Patients also help each other out. Those who are further along in the program can help those just starting out. Someone who has overcome a compulsion to wash his or her hands each time he or she touches money may be able to help someone else with a contamination obsession/cleaning compulsion. He or she may be able to explain how difficult it can be at first, but how it gets easier with time.

Most residential treatment programs have residents stay for one to three months. Residents practice ERP four hours a day on weekdays and two hours a day on weekends. Some activities are coached, but others are not, so that residents can get used to facing the anxiety themselves.

CONCLUSION

CBT has been shown to be very successful in treating OCD. It gets you to understand when a thought is an irrational OCD thought versus a real thought. It doesn't mean that your OCD will disappear forever. Instead, it teaches you strategies in waiting out your obsessions and anxiety until they pass. Over time, recognizing OCD thoughts and resisting ritualizing usually leads to a decrease in obsessions. Eventually, many teens are able to take back full control of their lives.

NOTES

1. Pat Miller, "Obsessive/Compulsive Dogs," *Whole Dog Journal* 4, no. 11 (November 2001): 3–5.

2. Fred Penzel, "Speaking about the Unspeakable: Breaking the Isolation for Teens and Young Adults" (lecture, Obsessive-Compulsive Foundation National Conference, Atlanta, GA, July 21, 2006).

3. Laurie Krauth, "Fear and Courage during Psychological Treatment of OCD," *OCD Newsletter* 19, no. 5 (Fall 2005): 1, 11.

4. William M. Gordon, "Need to Know OCD," *OCD Newsletter* 21, no. 1 (Winter 2007): 4.

5. Melanie Justice, psychotherapist, written correspondence with the author, July 28, 2007.

10 Getting Help by Using Medication

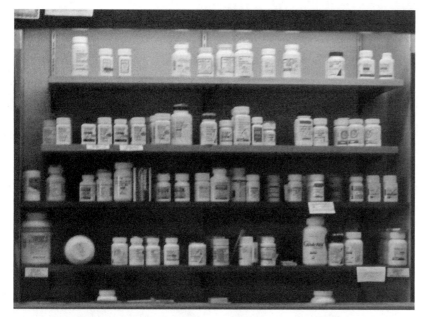

There are prescription medications for OCD. Your mental health professional can help to determine whether medication, CBT, or a combination of the two will be most beneficial. Photo by Natalie Rompella.

There are many medications used to treat OCD. Although none will cure your OCD, they can help make the symptoms less severe. When you see a mental health professional, he or she may discuss medications with you. Remember, only mental health professionals who have a medical degree can prescribe medicine. You may end up having to see two different health professionals to help you in different ways: one for medication and one for therapy.

> Besides [doing] little tricks, [since I was thirteen years old] I have been taking medicine prescribed by a psychiatrist. In the past I have taken Paxil [an SSRI], but it gave me constant headaches. Now I take Lexapro [also an SSRI], and the only negative side effect is sleepiness. Besides this minor setback, Lexapro has helped me considerably in alleviating my urges to count, and it has helped me become more comfortable around people in social settings (I have a little bit of social anxiety).—Claire, age nineteen

WHAT MEDICATIONS DO

There are two advantages to taking medications for OCD. First, they help neurotransmitters to work properly (see chapter 4). Different medication types help different neurotransmitters—some help primarily with serotonin amounts; others, with norepinephrine or dopamine.

Second, medications for OCD can help with depression that sometimes accompanies OCD. It is important to treat depression, especially if it is impacting your treatment. For instance, if you do not feel energized enough or you feel too overwhelmed to put in the effort required to perform CBT, you will not be able to fully engage in it. CBT requires a lot of patience and effort.

A PERSONAL STORY
Dieter, age thirty-nine

Similar to finding a therapist that specialized in OCD, it was also difficult to find a psychiatrist [who] specialized in monitoring meds for a patient with OCD. Ultimately, the medication was crucial because it helped manage the extraordinarily extreme levels of anxiety I felt as the result of the OCD. Once I was able to decrease that level of anxiety, I was able to begin doing CBT with the regularity and diligence that is necessary. Over time, I was able to decrease the medication. I still take medication, but have been steadily decreasing it over time.

When I was first diagnosed with OCD, I was very reluctant to take any meds because I had a general distrust of the mental health industry. Once I started taking meds, I eventually got over those concerns.

THE START OF MEDICATIONS FOR OCD

In 1980 the first medication was introduced to the United States to help lessen the symptoms of OCD. Clomipramine, an antidepressant marketed under the brand name Anafranil, first came out in Europe in the mid-1970s. Through careful study, scientists found that it also helped many patients with OCD reduce their obsessions and compulsions. Anafranil worked by helping to keep neurotransmitters such as serotonin (an imbalance of which is thought to be responsible for OCD) at the right level.

Since then, new medications have been found to be more effective for OCD and to have fewer side effects. In the mid-1980s medications called SSRIs became more commonly used to help lessen the symptoms of OCD.

SRIs AND SSRIs

For a long time, Anafranil was the only type of medication available for OCD symptoms. Anafranil is a serotonin reuptake inhibitor (SRI). Anafranil affects serotonin, as well as other chemicals in your brain. If your condition also requires changes in your levels of other neurotransmitters, such as norepinephrine, histamine, acetylcholine, and dopamine, you may be put on Anafranil. But if it doesn't, you may not want other chemicals in your brain affected, and because there are now more selective medications on the market, Anafranil is usually not recommended unless you have tried other ones and they have not helped.

Nowadays, most drugs used for OCD are SSRIs. They affect *only* the neurotransmitter serotonin. The most common SSRIs are Prozac (fluoxetine), Luvox (fluvoxamine), Zoloft (setraline), and Paxil (paroxetine). They are all antidepressants and antianxiety medications.

Different people's bodies react differently to these drugs, so one that works for someone else may not work for you. Your doctor can work with you to find the most effective medication. These medicines don't begin working right away; they sometimes take months to work. Some symptoms may even get worse before they get better. Remember: You're altering the chemical balance in your body. Your doctor can help in deciding whether a medication is or is not working for you.

Some medicines might cause your serotonin levels to be too high, causing your OCD to worsen. It might take a couple of changes in medicines or doses to get the right balance. Which drug to try first may depend on such factors as your family's history in using those medications, which drugs your insurance covers, and what side effects each drug has.

Unfortunately, you can't predict what will work without trying them. Be sure to take careful notes about how you are feeling, any side effects, and whether your OCD has improved or gotten worse since you began taking the medications. It will take patience, but don't give up. Just imagine how much better you'll feel when you do find the one that works for you.

If you are prescribed a medication, be sure that you take it as often as directed. It will not work properly if you forget to take it. (And, of course, never take more than the prescribed dosage

THE PPA

If you are unable to pay for medication, there is an organization that may be able to help you in finding an assistance program that offers you free or nearly free medication. The Partnership for Prescription Assistance (PPA) helps patients receive services by linking them to the appropriate source. The PPA will ask you about medications you take, your income, and your insurance. From there, the program will find whether the manufacturer of your medication can help out, whether there are discount cards available, or whether the state you live in has an assistance program. To find out more, go to www.pparx.org or call 1–888–4PPA-NOW.

and never share medication or borrow it from someone else.) It might help to keep your medication on your nightstand (where you'll see it when you wake up) or near your toothbrush. You should also let your doctor know about any other medications you are taking, even over-the-counter medicines, since there can be harmful drug interactions. When you get your prescription, read the pamphlet that comes with it. It will tell about any side effects and whether you should avoid caffeine or alcohol while taking it. (Of course, alcohol should always be avoided if you're underage.) Your doctor and your pharmacist can tell you anything else you should know about the drug.

Unfortunately, certain types of OCD do not respond as well to SSRIs. People with compulsive hoarding, scrupulosity, and pure O (pure obsessional, a type of OCD in which the person suffers only from obsessions and not compulsions) do not seem to benefit from SSRIs.[1]

ALTERNATIVES TO PILLS

Not everyone is able to swallow pills easily. Luckily, there are other options. For instance, Prozac also comes in a liquid form. Some pills can be crushed and mixed in with food (ask your pharmacist or doctor before you try this, since some pills must be swallowed whole). A pill can be put in applesauce and it will go down easier. Let your doctor know if this is an issue for you.

SIDE EFFECTS

You may not have a choice of which medication you take. And, as with taking any medication, you may experience side effects. Some common side effects of the SRI Anafranil are sleepiness, dry mouth (which can lead to tooth decay), and constipation. If you experience any of these, your doctor may be able to help you.

SSRIs also have side effects. Each has its own, but common side effects include sleepiness, insomnia, upset stomach, headache, and tremors. They can also cause sexual side effects, such as a decreased libido. Let your psychiatrist or doctor know if you are experiencing side effects; he or she may be able to help you reduce or better manage your symptoms. If one of the effects is too severe, you may need to switch to a different SSRI. Again, be sure to record how you are feeling throughout the day in case you need documentation.

Whatever you do, be sure to let the doctor know before you stop using any of the medications. For example, Paxil needs to be stopped gradually. Stopping suddenly can cause such symptoms as dizziness, nausea, and fatigue.

WILL YOU EVER GET TO STOP TAKING THE MEDICATION?

If you are relying solely on medication to control your OCD, if you were to stop taking the medication, your brain would return to the same mind games it played before. When you have completed CBT, on the other hand, you have trained your mind to stop obsessing. As discussed earlier, many doctors feel that CBT is more effective than medication. Research on which treatments work best for OCD also shows that CBT works best, followed by medications. However, people with more severe OCD, or who are also depressed, will usually need to take medication and undergo CBT. For those individuals, even after they complete their CBT treatment, some may be able to stop taking medication, others may not. It all depends on the person and his or her situation.

NOTE

1. Karen Cassiday, clinical psychologist and a founding fellow in the Academy of Cognitive Therapy, written correspondence with the author, September 2, 2006.

Other Treatments

One aspect of OCD is that it causes anxiety—anxiety about having an episode and anxiety when trying to avoid performing a compulsion. In addition, when you are anxious about something unrelated to your OCD, it can cause your OCD to flare up.

Learning how to relax is very important, whether you have OCD or not. There are many different ways to relax. Two of the most common are yoga and meditation. Practices such as meditation and acupuncture fall under the category of alternative medicine because they are alternatives to conventional medicine. When used in conjunction with conventional medicine, they are known as complementary medicine. Please note that although these other treatments can be helpful, they are not a substitution for professional help and/or ERP.

YOGA

Yoga is a form of exercise. Like other physical activities, yoga helps to release tension and thus causes your body to release chemicals called endorphins, which make you happier, more relaxed, and less stressed. Not only is yoga helpful because it is a physical activity, it also helps you to breathe properly: in through your nose, out through your mouth. This is called controlled breathing.

Yoga can be a great way to relax and feel less stressed. Photo courtesy of istockphoto.com/Eliza Snow.

MEDITATION

If you have trouble relaxing and often feel stressed, meditation might be very helpful to you. Meditation involves four main elements:

- Finding a quiet spot where you can't be distracted by such things as the television, other people, or noise. This is especially important for people just starting out.
- Sitting or lying down in a posture that is comfortable. It can also be done while standing or walking.
- Focusing your attention on an object, set of words, or your breathing.
- Letting distractions come and go without letting them impact you.[1]

Meditation is what is called a mind-body practice, since it has both a mental and a physical component. It can be used as complementary or alternative medicine. There are two main types of meditation:

◎ **Mindfulness meditation began in the ancient tradition of Buddhism. It enables you to be aware of what is presently happening, including the flow of your breath.**

◎ **Transcendental meditation originated in India. It has you concentrate on a mantra: a word, prayer, or sound that you repeat silently. This helps to avoid distracting thoughts (such as ones you have related to your OCD) so you can be fully relaxed.**

Before you begin a meditation program, you will want to let your health-care professional know. He or she may also be able to point you to local sources. In addition, there are books, videos, and Web sites on meditation, as well as places to attend classes. A great Web site from the National Center for Complementary and Alternative Medicine is http://nccam.nih.gov/health/meditation.

A SIMPLE MEDITATION EXERCISE

Turn off all screens (televisions and computers) and other noises in the room. Find a comfortable spot on a chair or on the floor. Place your hands on your lap with your palms up. Close your eyes or softly focus on an object. Try to focus your mind on your breath and think of something pleasant, such as the ocean. Imagine the sounds, sights, and feelings. Slowly breathe in and out.

PRAYER

Another method for relaxing is prayer. Many people find peace in talking with their creator and asking for strength. They feel they are getting support from a higher power. There are OCD support groups that focus on prayer. You may want to ask your health-care professional about local groups. In addition to sharing personal stories with one another, groups may share passages from the Bible or another holy book that are helpful in giving participants a sense of peace.

Please be advised that this may not be the best option for some: One form of OCD is scrupulosity, which involves repetitive prayer to rid oneself of guilt. If you suffer from this, you may not want to use prayer as a form of treatment.

ACUPUNCTURE

Acupuncture can look scary if you don't like needles, but you really barely feel them. Acupuncture, which is an ancient practice that originated in China, involves small needles that are inserted into the surface of the skin. All you feel is a little prick, and you usually don't even bleed from it.

The main use for acupuncture is to help alleviate pain in muscles and the skeletal system. It is also used for headaches, insomnia, and sinusitis. Acupuncture has also been used to help reduce anxiety and panic. If you plan to use this treatment, you will want to find a licensed acupuncturist.

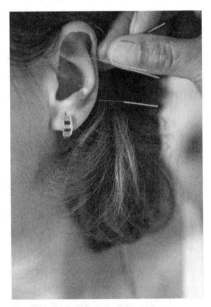

Acupuncture can be done all over your body or just on your ear, which is referred to as ear acupuncture or auricular therapy. Photo courtesy of istockphoto.com/Murat Koc.

BIOFEEDBACK

Another treatment to help relieve anxiety is called biofeedback. Biofeedback is a training technique that uses your own body's signals to help you relax and gain control over your body's emotional and physical reactions to stress. It is often used to relieve headaches and lower high blood pressure, as well as to

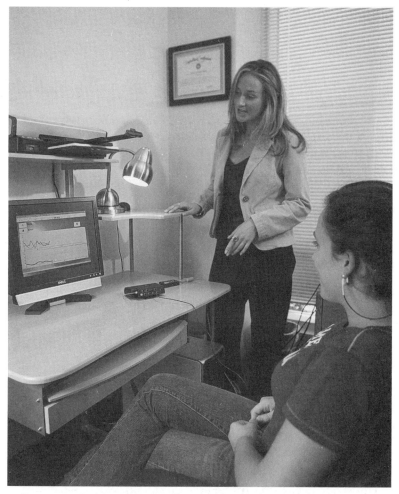

A biofeedback therapist explains results displayed on a monitor and teaches various techniques to manipulate and change these results. Patients can learn to gain control over their stress response, which will help them relax. Photo courtesy of the Institute for Personal Excellence, P.A., of Raleigh, North Carolina, by Wojtek Wojdynski.

A biofeedback therapist monitors activity and coaches the patient through the learning process at all times. Photo courtesy of the Institute for Personal Excellence, P.A., of Raleigh, North Carolina, by Wojtek Wojdynski.

regain movement lost by a stroke. Biofeedback practitioner Tami S. Maes explains how it works:

First, noninvasive sensors of the biofeedback device are attached to your skin's surface, typically on your fingers, neck, and head. The sensors gather and record your body's electrical activity. The device is also connected to a computer, which displays the results of your body's signals such as your sweat gland activity (called galvanic skin response—GSR), heart rate variability, skin temperature, and blood volume pressure. As you watch the monitor, you learn various relaxation techniques to help you control your reactions to stress and further lower your GSR, EMG [electromyography], and blood volume pressure while increasing your skin temperature in your peripherals (hands). A typical reaction to stress is cold hands. This is due to vasoconstriction of your blood vessels, which allows the blood to rush from your hands to your vital organs to protect your heart and lungs. Your eyes dilate so you are able to see better, and the blood also rushes to your skeletal muscles so you can run faster. These are all typical reactions to stress that leave your hand temperature cold. "Cold hands, warm heart" is the saying. With biofeedback you learn relaxation

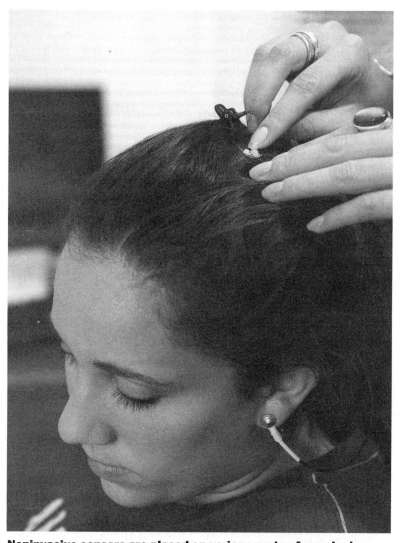

Noninvasive sensors are placed on various parts of your body. These sensors record the electrical activity of the body. When you are stressed, this activity changes. By recording and displaying these changes, the biofeedback therapist and the patient become aware of the impact of stress. A biofeedback therapist can teach you relaxation techniques during biofeedback training sessions so you are able to gain control over these responses. Witnessing this control for yourself further boosts your confidence and ability to control your stress before it controls you.[2] Photo courtesy of the Institute for Personal Excellence, P.A., of Raleigh, North Carolina, by Wojtek Wojdynski.

techniques to control these reactions to stress and increase vasodilatation in your hands to better circulate the blood throughout your body.

EMG is another modality of biofeedback that records electrical activity in the muscles. The higher the electrical activity, the more your muscles will feel tense. By working on decreasing the electrical activity, you can further release that tension, [and] you can learn to relax. This is especially important with OCD as you try to resist compulsions.

Neurofeedback works in the same manner as biofeedback using electroencephalography (EEG). With this modality, you can learn to regulate the electrical activity of your brain (or your brain waves) to feel better and function more efficiently. Typically, with anxiety, electrical activity in the brain is firing very rapidly and chaotic. By learning relaxation techniques and focusing drills, you are able to decrease this activity and further relax.[3]

EXERCISE

You probably already know about the health benefits of exercise: It helps your flexibility, it can get your heart pumping, and it can help burn fat and calories. But did you know it also helps your mind? Like yoga, exercise can release endorphins, causing you to be happier and reducing stress and anxiety. Not only that, when you are exercising, you may be able to get your mind off your OCD rituals.

"Exercise" is a broad term. If you think you don't like exercise, you probably just haven't found an activity you enjoy. There are team sports, such as football, basketball, and soccer. There are individual sports: tennis, badminton, golf, and bowling. Other activities include kayaking, weightlifting, and running. Another great form of exercise is dancing. There are so many kinds besides ballet and tap—many dance schools now teach hip-hop, belly dancing, and couples dances, such as swing, tango, and salsa.

ART THERAPY

Some clinics offer art therapy as an outlet for OCD. Art therapy is different from taking an art class in two major ways. First, it

Hiking is a great form of exercise that can help you relax and reduce stress and anxiety. Photo courtesy of istockphoto.com/Ben Blankenburg.

is not a class with a lesson. You are given studio time to work on a project in a medium of your choice. Art therapy is also different because rather than being taught by a teacher or professor, it is led by a person trained in helping people with mental health problems. Sometimes this person will work with your mental health professional and incorporate your exposure with response prevention into your art. For instance, if you have compulsions about contamination and are working on addressing this in your ERP, the art therapist may have you work in a medium that is a little uncomfortable for you, such as finger paint or clay.

The art therapist also works on redirecting you if your OCD flares up during your art therapy session. For example, he or she may notice that you are having perfectionistic tendencies and can help you work through that.

Art therapy can also be a way to express your emotions about OCD. The OCF National Conference has hosted exhibits of art created by people with OCD. Some pieces are unrelated to OCD; others express the artists' frustration and anger through serious pieces and cartoons.

While art therapy is mainly thought of as incorporating visual art, music and dance therapy may also be available to you.

WHAT TO AVOID

One way to help your OCD is to reduce anxiety. Although you can't change everything that happens in your life, you can make an effort to eat a healthy diet and avoid caffeine, sugar, and alcohol. Caffeine is a stimulant, causing anxiety by raising adrenaline. Avoid drinking coffee, caffeinated teas

STRESS AND STRESSORS

Can you believe that going on a vacation is considered a stressor, or an incident that can cause stress? Although vacations can be fun, large changes in your life can cause you stress.

Stressors can aggravate your OCD as well. Some common situations are the death of a friend or family member, having a baby or the birth of a new sibling, starting a new school, moving, going on a vacation, or having an illness.[4]

(herbal teas are usually caffeine free), soft drinks such as cola, and energy drinks.

Sugary foods affect blood sugar levels and can result in an initial surge, followed by a drop that triggers fatigue and difficulty concentrating. To avoid this problem, try to cut down on the amount of sugary foods you eat. Although alcohol is a depressant, it can also cause anxiety.

If you are taking an SSRI, you want to be sure to read the medication's pamphlet or ask your mental health professional about interactions. For instance, caffeine can cause problems when taken with Luvox, and with most medications, alcohol should be avoided.

NOTES

1. National Center for Complementary and Alternative Medicine, "Meditation for Health Purposes," http://nccam.nih.gov/health/meditation/overview.htm (accessed June 24, 2008).

2. Tami S. Maes, M.S., LRT, BCIA-C, biofeedback practitioner for Capital Biofeedback, Inc. of Raleigh, NC, written correspondence with the author, July 25, 2008.

3. Ibid.

4. Obsessive-Compulsive Foundation of Metropolitan Chicago [now OCD Chicago], "Causes," *How to Help Your Child: A Parent's Guide to OCD* [pamphlet] (Chicago, IL, 2006), 11.

12   **Related Disorders**

A PERSONAL STORY

Dan, age fifteen

I have both Tourette syndrome (TS) and OCD. TS is a neurological disorder that causes the afflicted person to perform uncontrolled movements and vocalizations. (The way I put it makes it sound like singing and dancing, but it comes off more annoying than entertaining.) OCD is another neurological disorder that causes obsessions and compulsions. An obsession is an irrational fear, such as a fear [of] germs on everyday objects, and a compulsion is an action the person feels they need to perform to prevent their imagined calamity, for example, washing one's hands repeatedly.

For me, Tourette shows up in the form of a vocal tic. I make a sound like repeated hums of the same pitch and tone, in rapid succession. I also make a soft groaning noise. I can suppress these noises briefly, but I cannot prevent them forever. Relaxing helps reduce the symptoms of Tourette ("tics"), and stress increases them. My OCD symptoms are hardly noticeable since I've gotten treatment, but before that they were very bad. I have the symmetry form of OCD, in which I have to "even up" things, like things I touch, light switches, and my own thoughts and speech. I also have a bit of contamination OCD, in which I feel the urge to avoid certain things that I think are too dirty, or seek reassurance that they are safe.

Decent people tend to politely state their queries about Tourette: "Excuse me, I couldn't help noticing your involuntary spasms. Could you enlighten me as to their purpose?" (I'm exaggerating.) Ruder people usually say, "Stop that, it's annoying!" Either way, my response is the same: "Sorry if I'm bothering you. It's a tic and I can't control it." If they haven't heard of Tourette, I give a brief explanation, but in my experience I've found that most people know what it is.

With OCD, it's another story. If a person with OCD is good at handling their symptoms, they probably won't even have to tell anyone about their OCD. OCD can be controlled, unlike Tourette. However, it's not easy. It takes a lot of ERP therapy—that is, exposure and response prevention. In this therapy style, the person with OCD is exposed to something that triggers their OCD, and then tries to prevent the response, i.e., the compulsion. Over several years of practicing what I learned in this therapy, I managed to get my OCD under control. If it shows, and anyone asks, I just say, "Sorry. I'll try to stop."

Many disorders are related to OCD; these are sometimes referred to as OCD spectrum disorders. These disorders can also occur along with OCD. When two or more disorders occur at the same time, they are called comorbid disorders. The following are some of the ones most commonly considered OCD spectrum and OCD comorbid disorders (professionals differ on which disorders they consider OCD spectrum disorders). Since this can get complicated, see the chart titled "Mental Disorders Related to OCD" in appendix B.

As you read different sections in this book, you might say to yourself, "I have this, too." It is not recommended that you make your own diagnosis. You may want to mention your concerns to a professional and let him or her diagnose you.

TOURETTE SYNDROME

Tourette syndrome (TS; also referred to as Tourette's disorder) can be comorbid with OCD. Some experts also believe it to be part of the OCD spectrum. This disorder involves tics, which are repetitive, uncontrollable movements. Motor tics can be actions, such as blinking and head jerking. Vocal tics involve the mouth, as in making clicking sounds or coughing. In rare cases, someone with TS has what's called coprolalia, which is a vocal tic in which the person curses uncontrollably.

TS is a neurological disorder (neurological means having to do with the nervous system). To be diagnosed with TS, a person must have signs of both motor and vocal tics for more than twelve months, and they must occur frequently throughout the day.[1] People can also have tics but not have TS. Since tics can occur more often when a person is under stress, learning ways to relax can make the tics occur less often. A therapist may also be able to help a person substitute one tic for another if the first is socially

MORE ON TS

A good Web site to visit for more information is the Tourette Syndrome Association at www.tsa-usa.org.

YOU GOTTA SEE THIS!

There are very few movies about OCD and TS. *dirty filthy love* is a British comedy about a man with both OCD and TS. You can find it in your local movie rental store in the comedy section, although it could also be classified as a drama. It shows how OCD can take over someone's life and, without treatment, cause much distress.

The movie also contains a PDF file you can view on your computer that shares interviews with the cast and the crew. One of the writers, Ian Puleston-Davies, actually suffers from OCD and used some of his own situations in the movie. *dirty filthy love* was released in 2005 by Granada International and is rated R for sexual content, language, and nudity.

---

unacceptable.[2] For example, if your tic involves spitting, your therapist might try to help you substitute blowing air from your mouth instead.

Some people with OCD also have tics. It can also be hard to distinguish a tic from an OCD action. Tics, however, are not done to get rid of anxiety. Instead, they happen involuntarily or are done to relieve a sensation the person is feeling. It is more common for someone with TS to have obsessions and compulsions than for someone with OCD to have TS.[3]

ASPERGER'S DISORDER (ASPERGER'S SYNDROME)

There are many disorders that have symptoms that resemble OCD. One is Asperger's Disorder (AD). AD is on the autism spectrum; its main symptoms include difficulty having relationships with others, odd and repetitive behaviors, and concentrated interest in limited areas. People with AD can have severe disabilities, but others live fairly regular lives. People with this disorder can have a lot of anxiety, but for different reasons than people with OCD.

One symptom of AD is rigidity. People with AD like sameness; they like a predictable schedule with a routine of timing and activities. They like things done a certain way and often have routines that cannot be changed without causing distress to them. Someone with OCD, on the other hand, may also have a routine, but it is part of the person's obsessions or compulsions. For instance, part of the routine of a person with OCD may be to touch the light switch four times. If the person were to change his or her routine by stopping it after two touches, it could cause anxiety. The person doesn't want to touch the light switch four times, but "has to." People with AD may need to do a repetitive task, such as lining up markers. Unlike people with OCD, however, they get enjoyment out of performing the task.[4]

If you notice someone crossing his or her arms in anger or beginning to cry, you may react to the person differently than if that person is smiling. People with AD may not be able to recognize the outward signs that show how people are feeling. People with AD often have trouble in social situations and may not make many friends. This is often because they have difficulty perceiving subtle social cues and reading nonverbal social gestures.

People with AD may also have difficulty expressing their thoughts orally. Oftentimes, they have an overly formal way of talking and acting in social situations. They can get anxious because they're aware they don't fit in well, but they don't know how to correct the situation.

Another characteristic of AD is an extreme interest in a particular topic, such as robots. To others this might look like an obsession, but the person with AD enjoys engaging in the topic repeatedly.

People with AD are at higher risk for getting OCD than the general public. Their obsessions and compulsions are just like those of OCD patients.[5]

AUTISM (OR AUTISTIC DISORDER)

Like AD, people with autism often have behaviors that look like OCD. Although they may engage in repetitive behaviors, they do this because of the sensory feelings they get, not because of anxiety. Autism is a disorder diagnosed by criteria that include not using nonverbal behaviors (such as making eye contact with others or using body language in social situations), not wanting to share interests with others, having a delay in speech, and using repetitive behaviors.

GENERALIZED ANXIETY DISORDER (GAD)

Another disorder that is often confused with OCD is called GAD. GAD is characterized by excessive worry and anxiety related to various events or activities—often everyday activities, such as worrying about getting to work on time or whether you got problems wrong on your homework. The diagnostic criteria for this disorder include having symptoms for at least six months and also suffering from physical symptoms such as restlessness, irritability, or difficulty sleeping.

Unlike with OCD, people with GAD worry about things related to their day-to-day activities. Although they have excess worry, there is a logical path to it, and they also often think that even though their worry makes them miserable, it serves a useful purpose. They believe it helps them manage problems or may even help them to prevent bad things from happening. Often people with OCD worry about things that don't have a logical path. For instance, a person with OCD may avoid the number three so that someone in his or her family doesn't get hurt. In addition, people with GAD don't perform the compulsive behaviors that, to some extent, help people with OCD alleviate the anxiety that they are feeling.

TRICHOTILLOMANIA

What are some things you do when you feel stress or anxiety? Some people bite their nails; others might smoke. People with trichotillomania (often referred to as trich—pronounced "trick"—or TTM) pull their hair: on their head, eyelashes, arms, or eyebrows. If you have this condition, you might agree that it doesn't just happen when you're stressed. Sometimes you may pull it when you're just sitting watching TV or reading a book. TTM is not a form of OCD but is an OCD spectrum disorder. It is called a body-focused behavior. Chronic skin picking—a condition called dermatillomania—is similar to TTM in which people may pick at a scab or their skin and feel pleasure or a release of anxiety after they have done it.

Like OCD, TTM is a biological condition. This means it doesn't happen from watching others or because you want it to—it's in your brain chemistry. There are two kinds of pulling that occur with TTM: focused and automatic. If you do focused pulling, you pull your hair when you're stressed or anxious. Automatic pulling happens when you are doing something else and you don't even realize you are pulling your hair. Some people also pull their hair when they're sleeping.

Although it is good to seek treatment, you might first want to keep track of when you are doing your pulling. Is it at school? When your parents are fighting? Or do you not notice doing it until you look down and see the hairs on your lap? Write this information down in a journal:

- date;
- time of day;
- activity doing while pulling occurs;
- stress level out of 10 (10 being the highest);
- where you pulled (hair on head, arms, etc.);
- for how long (thirty minutes, one hour, etc.); and
- what you did with the hair (did you look at it, bite it, etc.).

This information can help your therapist determine a treatment to prescribe for you.

Just as with OCD, CBTs have been shown to work best with TTM. As with OCD, SSRI medications may help with TTM but have not been shown to be effective in the long run at decreasing hair pulling or skin picking.[6] Since those with TTM may have comorbid disorders, helping the other conditions can help the TTM.

Relaxing is helpful with most anxiety disorders. Learning how to breathe slowly and properly, finding activities that help you unwind, and learning how to relax your muscles can help relieve your anxiety. Exercising is another good way to get rid of anxiety. As mentioned in chapter 11, it releases endorphins, which help you feel more relaxed and less stressed.

With TTM, your therapist may also teach you strategies for times you are feeling the urge to pull. He or she may recommend finding something to put in your hands that feels good and absorbs your feeling to pull. Squeezing stress balls, shaping putty, rubbing a smooth stone—you need to find what works for you. Getting your other senses involved can also help, so you might try looking at something appealing to you, lighting a nice-smelling candle, doodling, or listening to music. You want to make it past that moment when you feel you must pull.

If you pull without realizing it, knowing when you pull can help you know when to be more aware. For example, if you pull while watching TV, you will want to really work on keeping your hands busy during that time. If you pull during tests, you want to brainstorm good solutions with your therapist. Remember, stress can cause you to pull more often. Since you can't avoid all stress in your life, you want to work on ways to deal with stress.

Your therapist may talk to you about habit reversal training. This is a treatment in which the therapist will try to get you to do something that prevents you from pulling because you can't do both the competing action and the pulling at the same time. The therapist may start by role-playing a situation that would cause you to pull. You will try to do the other action instead of pulling. The goal is to get you to eventually notice when you are about to pull and be able to redirect your attention to something else.

It does not do any good to get mad at or punish yourself (or have others punish you). As you know, you don't like doing this and you don't mean to. You just need to find ways to be aware of what you do and work on ways to slowly stop.

In the meantime, you may feel embarrassed that you have missing hair. Possible solutions for women are to wear silk scarves or hats, or maybe even go to a hair stylist to find out about wigs. If you pull your eyelashes and you don't like how it looks, you may want to buy false eyelashes. They come in different lengths and you can get some that are more realistic looking. Missing eyebrows can be filled in with an eyebrow pencil. Most department stores have makeup counters where they can show you how to do it the first time to make them look more natural.

MORE ON TTM

A Web site to check out for information about TTM is www.trich.org.

If you are a male, you may be able to wear a hat in school if you explain the situation to the teacher. You may also choose to fill in missing eyebrows with an eyebrow pencil.

Caring and understanding friends can be quite supportive as you get through your treatment. They can help you to work through your anxiety as you resist your compulsion to pull or refocus your attention when you are feeling stressed.

Just as with OCD, this is a medical condition and you can get accommodations at school. See chapter 6 to learn more about laws regarding mental disorders in the context of school. If your TTM is causing you to pull because of the stress of exams, you may be able to take them in a different environment. If it is causing you to miss classes or lectures, you may be able to get copies of another student's notes or have a tutor. Whatever you do, do not let TTM stop you from reaching your goals.

DISORDERS RELATED TO TTM

Other disorders that involve similar compulsions to TTM are onychotillomania (compulsive nail picking), onychophagia (biting or chewing of fingernails), and rhinotillomania (compulsive nose picking).

BODY DYSMORPHIC DISORDER (BDD)

Another disorder that is related to OCD is BDD. People with BDD have an unrealistic image of themselves, sometimes feeling they are so unattractive or that a body part is so unsightly that they can't go out in public. The face is the area that people with BDD find most bothersome. Facial concerns include worries about wrinkles, blemishes, facial hair, and facial features (the size of their nose, lips, etc.). Other body parts people feel anxiety about are their genitals, stomach, thighs, and hands and feet. Men more commonly have a form of BDD called muscle dysmorphia, which focuses on not having enough muscle mass or not being strong enough. This can lead to exercising too much or the use of steroids.[7] People with BDD really see something different than reality when they look at themselves in the mirror.

BDD is thought to be related to low serotonin levels, making the cause biological. Much of the form BDD takes seems to have a cultural basis: Women are often shown in the media to be thin and flawless, and men are often shown to be muscular.

DID YOU KNOW?

It is estimated that 7 to 15 percent of people who get cosmetic surgery have BDD.[8]

BDD is similar to OCD because it causes people to obsess about "defects" that can be as small as a tiny birthmark. Their compulsion is to try to cover it up, avoid social situations, ask constantly for reassurance, look in mirrors, or groom religiously. A difference is that that people with OCD know that their thoughts and actions are unrealistic; people with BDD do not think their thoughts ("My nose is too big") and actions (cosmetic surgery) are unrealistic.

As with OCD, CBT and ERP are used as treatment. Working with a therapist, a person with BDD confronts situations that cause distress, such as looking in mirrors, trying clothing on in stores, and exposing the body part that causes anxiety (such as wearing shorts for someone who has anxiety about his or her legs). The therapist may even have the person exaggerate the distressing feature, such as wearing makeup in a way that accentuates it. SSRIs are also sometimes used in treatment.[9]

ANOREXIA AND BULIMIA

There is some overlapping between OCD and anorexia. Anorexia nervosa (often simply called anorexia) is an eating disorder that causes people to have a fear of becoming fat, so they often eat very little in hopes of losing weight. Of people with anorexia, 40 percent also have OCD.[10] Bulimia nervosa (often simply called bulimia) is also an eating disorder. It causes people to binge eat (eat an enormous amount of food) and then purge (force vomit, use laxatives or diuretics) or exercise to an extreme extent to get rid of the food/calories. (To be clinically classified, the behaviors need to have occurred at least twice a week for three months.)[11] These disorders can sometimes be a result of BDD as well.

Just like those who suffer from OCD, anorexics and bulimics perform actions to avoid something they are obsessed about, in their case, gaining weight. Those with anorexia have compulsions that include exercising, dieting, and weighing themselves. Those with bulimia feel the need to purge after binge eating.

As with BDD, the difference between the two disorders is that those with OCD know their thoughts are unrealistic, while those with anorexia or bulimia feel their thoughts are realistic. For instance, people with OCD may exercise because they feel if they don't, an unrelated action, such as their mother getting sick, might occur. Those with anorexia exercise because they believe they need to lose weight or that they will become fat if they don't exercise. Those with OCD usually also have insight: They know what they're doing is unreasonable or extreme. Those with anorexia or bulimia often have poorer insight and don't think what they're doing is unreasonable or extreme. They truly see themselves as overweight, regardless of whether they really are.

Treatments include CBT (sometimes including ERP), medication (such as antidepressants and/or SSRIs), and family therapy.[12]

IMPULSE CONTROL DISORDERS

There are other disorders sometimes confused with or related to OCD. Impulse control disorders are behaviors that cause a person to have an "itch" to perform a certain action, such as hair pulling. Once the person has performed the action, he or she feels a release of tension and anxiety. TTM is a type of impulse control disorder. Compulsive gambling and shopping are also sometimes put in this category. A difference between an impulse control disorder and OCD is that with impulse control disorder, the person gets some satisfaction after the action is performed, whereas with OCD the person feels a reduction in anxiety, but does not feel satisfied.

YOU GOTTA READ THIS!

Compulsive Acts: A Psychiatrist's Tale of Ritual and Obsession, **by Elias Aboujaoude**

This is a great book that focuses on OCD and impulse control disorders. Each chapter is about a patient whom the author, the director of the Impulse Control Disorders Clinic at Stanford University School of Medicine, has treated (of course, the details have been fictionalized). One patient had to avoid having objects too close to his nose, so he couldn't walk through doorways, shower (the shower head got too close to his nose), or use utensils. Other chapters include stories about patients with TTM, kleptomania, compulsive gambling, and what he calls "problematic Internet use." Not only does the book share facts on a variety of impulse control disorders, it also tells different treatments the doctor used for these patients.

SUBSTANCE ABUSE AND OCD

About 25 percent of people with OCD also have a substance use disorder (SUD), such as abusing alcohol or drugs.[13] Scientists are not sure what connection, if any, there is between the two disorders. It may be that the distress caused by OCD causes people to turn to drugs or alcohol hoping that it will relieve the anxiety they feel. (People with other forms of mental illness also often turn to alcohol and drug use.)

It is important for people with SUD and OCD to receive help for both. Some types of drugs may even make obsessions and compulsions worse. The treatment medications for OCD do not seem to help reduce problems with substance abuse. Instead there are specialized treatments, the first stage being detoxification. As with OCD, it is important to seek professional help for substance use disorders.[14]

OBSESSIVE-COMPULSIVE PERSONALITY DISORDER (OCPD)

Another disorder that is commonly confused with OCD is OCPD. Unfortunately, not as much is known about OCPD, but there are many theories. As you have read, OCD can be hereditary (genetic). OCPD is not believed to be genetic. Instead, it can be a result of modeling of the condition by a parent or guardian who had it and sometimes arises from a traumatic event in the person's life.

People with this disorder usually have some of the following traits:

◎ They are perfectionists: Things must be done just right. People with OCD might need to perform rituals in order to avoid a feeling, such as that harm will come to a loved one or to be a good person in the eyes of God (scrupulosity). People with OCPD, on the other hand, perform ritual actions because they feel it is the right way something should be done. Imagine writing an essay. A person with OCD might have the urge to cross a "t" just right because he worries that if he doesn't, someone will get sick. A person with **OCPD** will cross the "t" just right so that it looks perfect. Perfectionism can show up in how you dress, in your schoolwork, and in how you organize your room. It can also affect how you feel about other people. You may want to be friends only with people you don't find flaws in. This can also impact your relationships with the opposite sex. Do you have trouble finding someone worthy of dating you? It might be your perfectionism showing its ugly head.

- They think their way is the only way. Are you always right and everyone else is wrong? Related to this is thinking in black-and-white terms. People are either good or bad. You either like something or don't. You may have strong opinions.

- They may have issues with order. Things have to be exactly right. Do you line objects up or keep your pencil on an exact place on your desk? This is ordering. Again, there are symptoms of OCD that are very similar. To make a correct diagnosis, a therapist would need to talk to you about your reason for doing this.

Many people with OCPD don't want to get help because they see nothing wrong with their actions. They might see their ways as the right ways. A telltale sign of a problem is if you're having a hard time making and keeping friends. Maybe you have trouble finding a job that you're happy with. Most people with OCPD seek help for something else, such as OCD, and then find out they have OCPD as well. As with OCD, CBT and ERP may help you get control of your behaviors and rituals.

Only a professional can diagnose OCPD. If you feel that what you're reading here describes you to a *T*, bring that information with you to a professional. It is important that you have a good relationship with your therapist—you need to be able to trust your therapist to believe what he or she is saying. From there, you will probably begin CBT, helping you to realize that there is an in-between to your black-and-white thinking. You may have to do ERP: Doing something the *wrong* way and facing the consequence and anxiety.

Here are the differences between OCD and OCPD in a nutshell:

Obsessive-Compulsive Disorder	*Obsessive-Compulsive Personality Disorder*
Genetic	
Anxiety Disorder	Personality Disorder (Involves behavior that is inflexible and does not always follow what is expected by the culture. It begins in adolescence or early adulthood. It causes distress and/or impairment.)[15]
Perform rituals to avoid feeling anxiety.	Perform rituals because like things done properly.
Often are miserable dealing with behaviors/rituals related to OCD.	Don't see anything wrong with behaviors/rituals related to OCPD.

People with OCPD usually have perfectionistic tendencies. However, only a professional diagnosis can determine whether or not a person has OCPD. Photo courtesy of istockphoto.com/Stefan Klein.

YOU GOTTA READ THIS!

A great article on OCPD, "The RIGHT Stuff," by Steven Phillipson, PhD, can be found online at www.ocdonline.com/articlephillipson6.php.

COMPULSIVE HOARDING

Compulsive hoarding is sometimes considered a type of OCD, but some experts do not agree. Regardless, the treatment for compulsive hoarding is similar to that for OCD. Hoarding involves collecting objects to an extreme. These objects are often not even of value to the person who collected them.

Sometimes a person's hoarding compulsion can be obviously spotted; he or she may have a house or room that is filled to the brim with various items, leaving only a narrow path to walk.

IRRITABLE BOWEL SYNDROME

Another comorbid disorder with OCD is irritable bowel syndrome (IBS). This medical condition causes bloating, abdominal pain, diarrhea, and/or constipation. IBS is more common in people with anxiety disorders (as well as those with nonanxiety psychiatric disorders) than people without them. In a study done in 2006, it was found that 35 percent of the subjects with OCD surveyed also had IBS, in comparison with the 2.5 percent of the control group.[16] If you think you have IBS, you will want to let your therapist know, since this can affect which medication or dosage he or she may prescribe for you: SSRI medications may aggravate the condition.

Compulsive hoarders have a hard time getting rid of objects, such as books and papers. Photo by Natalie Rompella.

Others may hide their compulsion well, having placed their hoarded objects neatly in filing cabinets or plastic bins. People who hoard may not even realize it has become a problem; however, those around them likely will.

Hoarding is also thought to be linked to OCPD. Although it occurs in younger people, it might go unnoticed until things have a chance to pile up.

If you hoard, you may have been approached by friends or family members who have offered to "clean up" for you. If they did, chances are that eventually the spot they cleaned was back to its old ways again. Just as with OCD, hoarders need to work on changing their brain paths. They need to tell their brain it's okay to give away, throw away, and recycle items.

If you were to look at the items in your room right now, chances are you would see something in there that serves no purpose: an old stuffed animal, a pair of jeans at the back of your closet that you haven't worn for years, a dusty textbook. People hoard for different reasons. Some become emotionally attached to items. Maybe you got that stuffed animal when you were three and your favorite aunt took you to the carnival. When you look at the toy, it brings back all of those memories.

AUTHOR'S STORY

"I'm Shopping for Just One Thing"

Maybe you have a hard time going shopping without coming home with a cartful of stuff. Sometimes I go clothes shopping for a single item, such as a shirt of a certain color. I return with a pair of pants, socks, and two shirts. How could I not? They were on sale! Sales make items so tempting, people often buy things they wouldn't normally get.

Saving that stuffed animal is not the problem. The problem is if you've saved *all* of your stuffed animals, birthday cards, and childhood books because they bring back happy memories. It just becomes too much.

Regardless of why you save, if you feel your condition is a problem—or if those you live or work with find it a problem—you may want to get help.

Your therapist may have you do ERP. You will use baby steps in confronting objects that are attractive to you and either not buying them or getting rid of ones you have. At first it will be hard, but it will get easier with time.

Once your space is cleaned up, you'll want to think about a way to organize. Not everyone was made to organize in the same way. You may need to be more creative about where you put your things so that you actually follow a system. A great book on this is *Conquering Chronic Disorganization* by Judith Kolberg. In it, the author talks about how your personality can

AUTHOR'S STORY

An Easy Way to Waste a Day

As I was going through old college notebooks, at first I read every page again to see if it was important, tearing out ones I felt were. As I got further along, it became less important to me and I started skipping pages, and eventually I just tossed the notebook out.

shape whether you should use a filing system or find less conventional ways to organize. All that's important is that you choose something you can stick with.

Some people can't throw away or recycle items like newspapers and magazines because they are afraid they might throw out something valuable they wrote that might have gotten mixed into the clutter. If you seek help for your hoarding, you'll want to tell your therapist what you hoard, where it is, and your reason for collecting it. This can help with how you are treated. You should understand that to stop being a hoarder, you are going to be asked to get rid of items. This will be difficult and painful, but think of all the benefits you will have: a clean and organized home, as well as a space where you can have family and friends visit.

Organizing

As you clean up, you'll need to come up with an organizing system that works for you. First, make a list of possible ways to organize the area. For instance, with clothing, you may first want to sort through: wear and never (or rarely) wear (and put a Post-it on each item you never wear and why). Look at your reasons for keeping your "nevers." Be realistic about whether they are valid reasons. Is "I wore that when I won a writing contest" a good reason to keep it? Maybe you also have a picture of this event; that might be a better way to remember. You may have clothes that are too small or large. Donate or throw away as many "nevers" as you can. Box up the rest with a label, such as "one size too small," so that if you need them you can easily find them.

AUTHOR'S STORY

Parting with the "Skinny Day Jeans"

I had trouble parting with a pair of jeans that I was able to squeeze into when I lost a lot of weight—I finally faced the fact I will never fit into them again and I don't need the jeans around to remember my weight loss.

AUTHOR'S STORY

How I Got Organized

After years of trying to use a file cabinet for my papers, I finally realized it didn't work for me. I would stack all "papers to be sorted" on top of the cabinet rather than find the folder they belonged in. I realized that I like to have my papers in plain view. Now I have thirty or so stacking trays with labels on them. I can easily slip the papers in the appropriate slot and can "see" everything easily. I am also not limited to the narrow space a file folder allows, and I can move the papers away out of sight. Since I use Post-it labels for each tray, I can effortlessly get rid of a category if I no longer need it.

I also have a problem getting rid of old clothes. As I pulled some items out of my closet that I hadn't worn in a long time, I thought about why I was keeping them. One I wore the night I met my husband; another reminded me of my old apartment. I told myself, "Not good reasons!"

I decided to sort through my closet—I made labels for categories for clothes that I hadn't worn in a while:

- out of style
- too small or large
- too youthful
- worn or stained
- unflattering
- tired of it
- try on again

I put the labels on the floor, and I then threw each item into one of these piles. Then, before I lost my nerve, I tried on all the items in the last category. I realized I just wasn't ready to part with some, even though I doubted I would really wear them. I am putting them in my trial period drawer. I will try to wear them within two weeks; otherwise, I will part with them.

I was finally ready to get rid of all my other piles. I combined them and resorted by winter and summer clothes. I planned to donate the summer clothes right away and put the winter clothes in a marked box that would be ready to take to a resale shop in a couple of months.

By first sorting by reason, I didn't feel that I was officially getting rid of the clothes and it made it easier. I did this alone, but it might be easier to have a friend nearby to help you say "out of style," "unflattering," or "*I'll* wear that!"

With the items you are keeping, brainstorm different ways to organize the items: by color, by item (skirts, pants, shirts), by dressiness, by how often worn, and so on. Decide which system works best for you. Realize that whatever way you were taught to organize your items may not work for you—you need to think outside the box.

NOTES

1. American Psychiatric Association, *Diagnostic and Statistical Manual of Mental Disorders*, 4th ed., text revision (Washington DC: American Psychiatric Association, 2000), 111, 114.

2. Tourette Syndrome Association, "Tourette Syndrome: Frequently Asked Questions," www.tsa-usa.org/Medical/Faqs.html (accessed July 20, 2008).

3. Tamar E. Chansky, *Freeing Your Child from Obsessive-Compulsive Disorder* (New York: Crown, 2000), 75.

4. Fugen Neziroglu and Jill Henriksen, "Differentiating between Asperger's and Obsessive-Compulsive Disorder," *OCD Newsletter* 19, no. 2 (Spring 2005): 1, 12–13.

5. Karen Cassiday, clinical psychologist and a founding fellow in the Academy of Cognitive Therapy, written correspondence with the author, January 2, 2008.

6. Ibid.

7. Elana Golan, "Update on a Spectrum Disorder: Body Dysmorphic Disorder," *OCD Newsletter* 20, no. 2 (Spring 2006): 7, 15.

8. Golan, "Update on a Spectrum Disorder," 7.

9. Fugen Neziroglu and Alicia Slavis, "Gosh, I Dislike the Way I Look," *OCD Newsletter* 20, no. 5 (Fall 2006): 3.

10. Eda Gorbis and Jenny C. Yip, "OCD and Anorexia," *OCD Newsletter* 20, no. 5 (Fall 2006): 4.

11. APA, *Diagnostic and Statistical Manual*, 594.

12. Gorbis and Yip, "OCD and Anorexia," 4–5.

13. David H. Barlow, "Anxiety Disorder, Comorbid Substance Abuse, and Benzodiazepine Discontinuation: Implications for Treatment," National Institute on Drug Abuse, www.nida.nih.gov/pdf/monographs/monograph172/033-051_Barlow.pdf (accessed November 11, 2007).

14. Jon E. Grant and Suck Won Kim, "Management of Substance Use Disorders in Obsessive Compulsive Disorder," *OCD Newsletter* 20, no. 4 (Summer 2006): 1, 3.

15. APA, *Diagnostic and Statistical Manual*, 685.

16. Masand Prakash, N. J. Keuthen, et al. "Prevalence of Irritable Bowel Syndrome in Obsessive-Compulsive Disorder," *CNS Spectrums* 1 (January 11, 2006): 21–25.

13 Support Groups

A PERSONAL STORY

Michelle, age sixteen

Having suffered from OCD myself, I have some advice and things to keep in mind for fellow sufferers: finding the right therapist trained in CBT, [finding] a psychopharmacologist specializing in OCD in teens, and doing ERP as much as possible are key ingredients for recovery. However, none of these will help you in your recovery unless you, yourself, are motivated to do the hard work involved. I have learned that OCD is not something I asked for, and it is not my fault for having it. I found that instead of dwelling on the unfairness that I have this disorder, it is a much better use of energy to channel my frustration into fighting my OCD. I saw how OCD truly is a "family disease," and the toll it took on my family. However, they did not consider me a burden; instead, they were just sad because when one member is suffering, everyone struggles. I also experienced the isolation and embarrassment that often comes with having OCD. Meeting other teens with OCD made a world of a difference for me, and this can be accomplished by joining an OCD support group, or even starting one if there is not a group in your area. Make sure that you find a support network for yourself, such as true friends, family, others with OCD, or doctors.

It is also important to understand that fighting OCD takes a lot of motivation and is probably one of the hardest things—if not the hardest thing—you will have to overcome. It is a lifelong battle. In the end, it was really only me that could force myself to do an exposure. However, I started in tiny steps, and was soon able to tackle harder things as my confidence increased when I started having even just a little success. Going through therapy, reading about OCD, and listening to the experts on the topic really taught my family and me a lot, and we are now all able to recognize (and refrain from doing) the things that we were carrying out to accommodate my OCD. Most importantly, though, just try to keep hope even when times are tough, and know that there is a light at the end of the tunnel.

ONLINE CHAT GROUPS AND LISTSERVS

There are many different ways to chat with others who have OCD. Yahoo! has a site that features many different OCD Listservs. If you go to http://groups.yahoo.com, you can use keywords to search for groups. After reading about the group, you can click the "Join This Group" button and get e-mails each time someone responds or once a day (daily digest), or go to the group's Web site to read all of the entries.

Some of the Web sites include http://health.groups.yahoo .com/group/newocdteen, a group for teens that is moderated by OCD doctors. This moderation means that the doctors block inappropriate responses and offer their advice when needed. Another is http://health.groups.yahoo.com/group/ obsessivecompulsivedisorder3, for all people with OCD (not necessarily just teens). There is also a group for parents of children with OCD, at http://health.groups.yahoo.com/ group/ocdandparenting. This group is moderated by OCD professionals. Another group, at http://health.groups.yahoo .com/group/ocdstudent, is for students age eighteen to twenty-five who have OCD.

Because you are communicating with total strangers from around the world, you never want to give out any personal information on these Listservs. Unfortunately, there are predators out there who don't have your best intentions in mind. Never agree to meet up with anyone you don't know or give identifying information to someone you're not sure you can trust. You do not want to give your e-mail address, home address, phone numbers, or last name. You don't even need to use your real name if you don't want to. When you sign up, you can have your e-mail address hidden, or you can create a free account to use instead of your regular e-mail address.

Through the Listserv you can ask others questions about thoughts they've had, medications they've tried, and different treatments they've experienced. Some people never even ask questions; they just read the conversations of others, which is fine, too.

THE OBSESSIVE-COMPULSIVE FOUNDATION (OCF)

In 1986 a group of people with OCD decided to increase awareness of the disorder by the public. They were all participants in a study done on a new medication for OCD called Luvox. After the study, Dr. Wayne Goodman, now professor and chair of the Department of Psychiatry at the University of Florida College of Medicine, thought it was a good idea for some of the study participants to form an OCD support group.

But this group wasn't satisfied with simply supporting one another; they decided to raise awareness about OCD by sending a letter to the popular television news program *20/20*. The program aired a report sharing the story of one of the group members. Members of the OCF, which the group now had formed, asked for the name of the foundation to be included in the credits. As a result, the OCF received thousands of letters from people suffering from OCD or who had a family member struggling with it.

The OCF created a question-and-answer brochure on OCD, and started the *OCD Newsletter*, which shares the latest information on OCD.[1]

The OCF, a national organization for OCD with more than six thousand members, continues to grow. To learn more about the organization, visit www.ocfoundation.org.

NATIONAL CONFERENCE

Every summer the OCF holds a conference for people with OCD and family members wanting to help those with OCD. The conference has sessions with experts offering information on the latest treatments. In addition, there are sessions just for teens. For more information, go to www.ocfoundation.org.

LOCAL SUPPORT GROUPS

Many cities have organizations for people with OCD. These are usually run by doctors or therapists who can guide groups in their discussions. Each person in the group may share how

---

AUTHOR'S STORY

My Personal Experience at the OCF Conference

One of the workshops on contamination started out with the attendees sitting on the floor. It ended with them eating ABC gum (that's "already been chewed" gum). Now, understand that I have trouble looking at my own chewed gum, but watching people eat already chewed gum was too much—I gagged.

As I mentioned in the foreword, although I went to the conference for the purpose of research, I benefited from all the information I received. I attended sessions on ERP, hoarding, information hoarding, the transition to college, contamination, cell phone ERP, mental compulsions, trichotillomania, and obsessive-compulsive personality disorder. There were also sessions for teens that were closed to adults, sessions for kids, and sessions giving information on the genetics of OCD, insomnia, and sexual obsessions—there was definitely something for everyone.

The mood at the conference was positive. There were activities to help participants relax, such as art therapy that let people create things with a variety of media. There was also an art gallery with art done by people with OCD. In the evening, there were support groups one night, and a dinner reception and a movie (complete with popcorn) on OCD the second night. It seemed as if others viewed it as encouraging as I did; for some people I talked to, this was their first experience being around other people who also had OCD. Since some people brought their families with them, it was also a chance for their support teams to meet other support teams.

OCD affects his or her life. Each member may then choose a facet of his or her OCD to focus on before the next meeting.

At a support group, each week members share whether they met their goal. If they did, a new goal is set.

OBSESSIVE COMPULSIVE ANONYMOUS

Another group that can be helpful to make it through this process is a local Obsessive Compulsive Anonymous (OCA) group. You might have heard of Alcoholics Anonymous (AA) chapters that provide support for people in recovery from

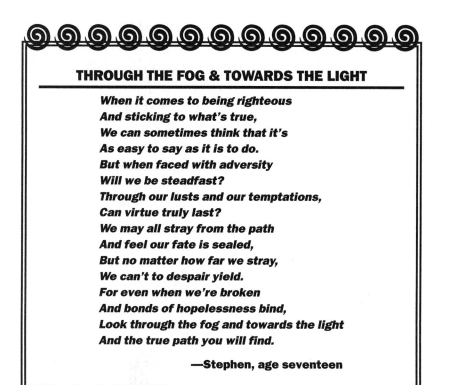

THROUGH THE FOG & TOWARDS THE LIGHT

*When it comes to being righteous
And sticking to what's true,
We can sometimes think that it's
As easy to say as it is to do.
But when faced with adversity
Will we be steadfast?
Through our lusts and our temptations,
Can virtue truly last?
We may all stray from the path
And feel our fate is sealed,
But no matter how far we stray,
We can't to despair yield.
For even when we're broken
And bonds of hopelessness bind,
Look through the fog and towards the light
And the true path you will find.*

—Stephen, age seventeen

alcoholism; OCA provides a place for people with OCD to find the same support. OCA follows a twelve-step program, as discussed in the OCA manual, *Obsessive Compulsive Anonymous—Recovering from Obsessive Compulsive Disorder*. Meetings focus on discussing the twelve steps, reading and talking about a story from the manual, examining a common issue related to OCD recovery, and allowing group members to share their

WEBZINES

At the OCF Web site, you can go to www.ocfoundation.org/organizedchaos to read the webzine *Organized Chaos*. It features articles and poems written by teens about their experience with OCD. In addition, you can submit your own articles and poems for publication.

personal experiences with OCD and discussing them as a group. OCA meetings are not counseling sessions. They are run by members of the group, rotating the leader. The belief is that it should not be just one person's meeting—everyone benefits.

Like AA, each member is sponsored by someone who has had some recovery. Sponsors are there as a support for a member, to try to help him or her maintain growth. For more information on Obsessive Compulsive Anonymous, go to its Web site at http://obsessivecompulsiveanonymous.org/.[2]

NOTES

1. Patricia Perkins, executive director, OCF, written correspondence with the author, November 12, 2007.

2. Roy C., "OCA—A Place for Healing," *OCD Newsletter* 19, no. 5 (Fall 2005): 5.

14 Conclusion

If this is the first book you have read about OCD, you might find that it threw a lot of information at you all at once. Here is a condensed version of the facts that are most important to remember.

More than 5 million people in the United States have symptoms of OCD. Not all people who have suffered from the disorder have received help. One reason is that in the past, doctors knew less about the disorder and didn't offer the proper help they can now. OCD is no longer an unknown disorder—more and more research is being done that gives doctors a clearer picture of it, as well as finding treatments that will alleviate the symptoms.

OCD is a biological disorder. It is not a result of how you were raised and is not caused by an event, but it can be set off by environmental triggers, such as a traumatic event. It can also flare up when you haven't slept well, aren't eating right, or are stressed. OCD can begin when you are a child, an adolescent, or an adult. Some children begin having OCD symptoms after having strep throat. This less common type of OCD is called PANDAS.

There are many types of OCD. One of the most common forms is the obsession with contamination and the compulsion to clean. Another form involves becoming obsessed with the thought that you have left an appliance on or a door open and having the compulsion to check over and over. Other people count, touch, or repeat actions or thoughts. Hoarding is an action that is included in both OCD and OCPD. People who hoard collect objects or information to an extreme or dysfunctional degree.

Less common or less talked about forms of OCD include the following:

- ◎ **scrupulosity (praying to avoid harm);**
- ◎ **arranging; and**
- ◎ **having unwanted thoughts, such as about harming others or having inappropriate or unwanted sexual relations.**

Often people with OCD do not have only one form of OCD; for instance, someone may have unwanted thoughts *and* an obsession about contamination. OCD often makes people have fears of doing harm to someone or something they really care about.

OCD is not a new disorder; it is believed to have affected people as far back as the ninth century. However, it is only recently that OCD was recognized as an anxiety disorder.

OCD is believed to be genetic. Those with OCD often have a relative who has it as well (although the type of OCD may differ). OCD is caused by parts of the brain being overactive or not functioning the way they should. Too many messages, or false messages, are being sent through. In addition, people with OCD may not have enough of the neurotransmitter serotonin traveling from the brain to the central nervous system. By performing ERP, people can train their brains to work more effectively.

Your personal, school, and professional life can be affected by your OCD. It can impact you at work, making you late or unable to perform your duties because of the compulsions you are performing. It can cause similar problems in school: Obsessive thoughts can impede your learning, make you late for class, or cause you to miss sleep, to name a few. Luckily, public schools are required to make accommodations for students with disabilities, including such adjustments as more time to complete tests or having physical education the last period of the day. Even in college, you can receive help so that your OCD doesn't run your life. The amount of sleep you get and your sleep patterns can also impact your OCD, so try to get the recommended amount of sleep for your age and go to bed around the same time each night and get up at the same time each morning.

Some people are able to hide their OCD in public but then have a major blowup when they get home, compulsively scrubbing or counting. It is important that your family members know how they can help you rather than enabling you. Siblings might have a hard time understanding your situation and may need counseling, too.

Most people with OCD need the help of a mental health professional. People with OCD might see a psychologist for therapy, or a psychiatrist, who can prescribe medication. Sometimes they may see both. Even if you don't live near an expert on OCD, you can receive help. Many therapists are willing to do some sessions over the phone.

One of the main types of therapy an expert will use for OCD is CBT. CBT involves learning about your triggers and not falling prey to what your mind is falsely telling you to think or do. Part of this therapy is often ERP. In ERP, your therapist will have you do or think about situations that produce anxiety while refraining from ritualizing. You would work your way up from easier situations to more anxiety-producing situations. When you do this, your mind starts to habituate and not react so strongly, leading to decreased anxiety levels and a decreased need to perform compulsions.

Medications are also sometimes used to help people with OCD. However, medications will not cure OCD. Instead, they are often prescribed for people who cannot participate in CBT due to extreme anxiety or depression. There are two main kinds of medication used for OCD: SRIs, which affect various neurotransmitters in the brain, and SSRIs, which focus on the neurotransmitter serotonin. These are prescription-only medications. Often it is a matter of trial and error to discover which one is right for you. You should never share or borrow someone else's medication.

There are some people with OCD for whom neither CBT nor medication is enough. Their situation is so severe that they cannot function in a healthy way. There are intensive treatment programs across the United States that can benefit such people. A therapist can assist you in knowing whether this is something you need to do, as well as in choosing which program is the best for your situation.

In addition to therapy, there are activities you can partake in to help you relax, such as yoga and meditation. Exercise can also aid in calming the mind. You might already know which activities help you relax—for instance, dancing might work for some, while running might work for others.

There are a number of other disorders related to OCD:

- ◎ **TS involves repetitive, uncontrollable movements called tics.**
- ◎ **People with AD or autism are often thought to also have OCD because they sometimes perform activities repetitively.**
- ◎ **TTM is a disorder that causes people to pull their hair out.**
- ◎ **BDD causes those who have it to feel that they are so unattractive they can't go out in public.**
- ◎ **Anorexia is a disorder that causes people to think they are overweight. They then diet excessively to lose weight (anorexia nervosa) or they binge and purge to get the food out of their body (bulimia nervosa).**
- ◎ **Habit and impulse control disorders make people perform repetitive actions for no apparent reason.**
- ◎ **OCPD is different from OCD in that it is a personality disorder rather than an anxiety disorder. People who have it like things to be orderly and are often said to be perfectionists.**
- ◎ **Compulsive hoarding is sometimes said to be a form of OCD; other times it is said to be a disorder related to OCD. People who have it collect items that are often thought of by others as useless or unneeded.**

Some people with OCD benefit from joining a support group. Sometimes the group is a mix of people with various anxiety disorders; others are solely for people with OCD. Attending a support group gives members a chance to talk about how OCD impacts their lives and to offer one another support. Members set goals for themselves that they work on in between sessions.

A PERSONAL STORY
Mariah, age seventeen

At the age of fourteen I went to a residential treatment center in Utah, far away from my life and family. Along with OCD and anxiety, I was also struggling with self-injury. It was not until I was hospitalized at the age of seventeen that I made the connection between my self-injury and OCD. I was completely unable to control my thoughts (just like everyone else), and cutting gave me a sense of control; it was something I could be "perfect" at. It also relieved the tension and anxiety that I carried around every day—it became a distraction and gave me something to focus on rather than my anxiety.

While I was stabilizing my self-injurious behaviors at the hospital, I also learned how to reduce my anxiety and take control over my OCD. Exposure therapy and cognitive behavior therapy were extremely helpful for me. Because my physical OCD rituals had been largely minimized with the help of medication, we focused mostly on my obsessive thoughts. Although I had not had intrusive sexual thoughts for about three years, I was still afraid that the thoughts would come back, and was avoiding people who were not "right" and performing breathing rituals to prevent the thoughts. After discussions with both my therapists and my mother, we deduced that I was experiencing anticipatory anxiety, because of my fear that the thoughts might occur. So I started working with therapists to face my fears and essentially reduce my anxiety and OCD rituals. They had me face my biggest fear—which was to actually sit down and think sexual thoughts about people I didn't like. It was extremely uncomfortable at first, and it was difficult not to perform breathing rituals or "wipe it off," but after time I was able to relax and realize that the thoughts could not hurt me.

During exposures and in real situations where I feel anxious and have the urge to perform OCD rituals, it helps to remind myself that nobody can control their thoughts, no thought can be "bad," and just because I think something, it doesn't mean I want it to happen or that it will happen. Constantly reminding myself of the facts helps me to not blame myself for having intrusive sexual thoughts, and allowing them to pass without feeling the need to perform rituals to make them go away. Without exposures and CBT exercises, I would still be afraid of my own mind, and unaware of how to cope with anxiety-provoking situations.

I'm coming to terms with the fact that I will always have OCD and anxiety, but also that it does not make me a bad person. While taking medication has helped reduce my anxiety, learning how to respond to uncomfortable situations on my own has been incredibly beneficial. It has helped me to take control over my OCD and over my life again.

Also helpful are online chat groups and Listservs for people with OCD. What's nice about this is that you don't need to leave home and can remain anonymous. Lastly, local and national conferences and workshops allow you to know about the latest types of therapy for OCD.

A couple of the most important points of this book are that you are not alone and that help is available. If you haven't told

ACRONYMS TO REMEMBER

Here is a cheat sheet of various acronyms used throughout the book. It might be helpful to know these if you plan to do any browsing on the Internet. They are also all listed in the glossary.

ADA: Americans with Disabilities Act
ADHD: attention-deficit/hyperactivity disorder
CBT: cognitive behavioral therapy or cognitive behavior therapy
DSM-IV-TR: *Diagnostic and Statistical Manual of Mental Disorders* (4th ed., text revision)
ECT: electroconvulsive therapy
ERP: exposure with response prevention
IDEA: Individuals with Disabilities Education Act
IEP: Individualized Education Program
OCD: obsessive-compulsive disorder
OCPD: obsessive-compulsive personality disorder
PANDAS: pediatric autoimmune neuropsychiatric disorders associated with streptococcal infections
PET: positron emission tomography (scans)
SRI: serotonin reuptake inhibitor
SSRI: selective serotonin reuptake inhibitor
TTM: trichotillomania

your parents yet, it might be time to. Seeing a health professional doesn't make you "crazy"—it might be the only way to help lessen your OCD. Who else you tell is up to you.

You've read a lot of passages from teens with OCD. Some teens were just beginning their journey and still expressed their pain. Others were on the up end and shared how treatment really helped them. Now it's your turn. It's your chance to start your journey. If you've read this far, you know it's going to take hard work, but you can do it. You can knock OCD down and take back your life.

Appendix A: Great Sources

There are some great resources out there. Some are eye-opening; others are humorous. The books and Web sites below are just some of the sources available.

A very helpful guide with up-to-date information is the *OCF Newsletter*. Members of the OCF (the national organization for OCD) receive newsletters through the mail, with articles written by professionals about the newest studies done on OCD and OCD spectrum disorders. Visit the OCF's Web site to find out more: www.ocfoundation.org.

BOOKS

Nonfiction

Aboujaoude, Elias. *Compulsive Acts: A Psychiatrist's Tale of Ritual and Obsession*. Berkeley: University of California Press, 2008.

American Psychiatric Association. *Diagnostic and Statistical Manual of Mental Disorders*, 4th ed., text revision. Washington, DC: American Psychiatric Association, 2000.

Baer, Lee. *The Imp of the Mind*. New York: Dutton, 2001.

Bell, Jeff. *Rewind, Replay, Repeat: A Memoir of Obsessive-Compulsive Disorder*. Center City, MN: Hazelden, 2007.

Chansky, Tamar E. *Freeing Your Child from Obsessive-Compulsive Disorder*. New York: Crown, 2000.

Colas, Emily. *Just Checking*. New York: Pocket Books, 1998.

Deane, Ruth. *Washing My Life Away: Surviving Obsessive-Compulsive Disorder*. London: Jessica Kingsley, 2005.

Kant, Jared Douglas, with Martin Franklin and Linda Wasmer Andrews. *The Thought That Counts: A Firsthand Account of One Teenager's Experience with Obsessive-Compulsive Disorder*. New York: Oxford University Press, 2008.

Kolberg, Judith. *Conquering Chronic Disorganization*. Decatur, GA: Squall Press, 2004.

March, John S. *Talking Back to OCD*. New York: Guilford Press, 2007.

Obsessive Compulsive Anonymous. *Obsessive Compulsive Anonymous: Recovering from Obsessive Compulsive Disorder*. Williston Park, NY: Aden Graphics, 1990.

Rapoport, Judith. *The Boy Who Couldn't Stop Washing*. New York: Dutton, 1989.

Summers, Marc. *Everything in Its Place: My Trials and Triumphs with Obsessive Compulsive Disorder*. New York: Jeremy P. Tarcher/Putnam, 1999.

Traig, Jennifer. *Devil in the Details: Scenes from an Obsessive Girlhood*. New York: Little, Brown, 2004.

Wells, Joe. *Touch and Go Joe: An Adolescent's Experience with OCD*. London: Jessica Kingsley, 2006.

Fiction

Chappell, Crissa-Jean. *Total Constant Order*. New York: Katherine Tegen Books, 2007.

Dolley, Chris. *Resonance*. Riverdale, NY: Baen Books, 2005.

Harrar, George. *Not as Crazy as I Seem*. Boston: Houghton Mifflin, 2003.

Hesser, Terry Spencer. *Kissing Doorknobs*. New York: Laurel Leaf, 1999.

Niner, Holly. *Mr. Worry: A Story About OCD*. Morton Grove, IL: Albert Whitman, 2004. [see brothers and sisters section in chapter 7]

Talley, Leslie. *A Thought Is Just a Thought: A Story of Living with OCD*. Brooklyn, NY: Lantern Books, 2004. [see brothers and sisters section in chapter 7]

Tashjian, Janet. *Multiple Choice*. New York: Scholastic Signature, 1999. [see brothers and sisters section in chapter 7]

Wagner, Aureen Pinto. *Up and Down the Worry Hill*. Deerfield Beach, FL: Lighthouse Press, 2004. [see brothers and sisters section in chapter 7]

MOVIES AND TELEVISION SHOWS

Breckman, Andy. *Monk* (television show). Directed by Dean Parisot. Universal City, CA: Universal Studios, 2002.

The House of the Obsessive-Compulsives (television documentary). Executive Producers: Syeda Iritazaali, David Granger; Series Producer: Andrew O'Connell. London: Monkey Kingdom, 2005.

Logan, John. *The Aviator* (DVD). Directed by Martin Scorsese. Burbank, CA: Warner Home Video, 2005.

Pope, Jeff, and Ian Puleston-Davies. *dirty filthy love* (DVD). Directed by Adrian Shergold. New York: Hart Sharp Video; Sundance Channel Home Entertainment, 2004.

WEB SITES

ADA Home page, www.ada.gov. Provides information on the Americans with Disabilities Act.

Yahoo! Groups, http://groups.yahoo.com. Yahoo! Groups allows you to search for Listservs on a variety of topics, such as OCD, TS, or TTM. Here are some of the Yahoo! Groups that deal with OCD:

newocdteen, http://health.groups.yahoo.com/group/ newocdteen. A Yahoo! Group for teens with OCD that is moderated by OCD doctors.

obsessivecompulsivedisorder3: Support for Those Affected with OCD, http://health.groups.yahoo.com/group/ obsessivecompulsivedisorder3. A Yahoo! Group for people with OCD (not just teens).

The OCD and Parenting List, http://health.groups.yahoo .com/group/ocdandparenting. A Yahoo! Group for parents of children with OCD; it is moderated by many OCD professionals.

ocdstudent: Support for Students with OCD, http://health
.groups.yahoo.com/group/ocdstudent. A Yahoo!
Group for students between the ages eighteen and
twenty-five who have OCD.

National Center for Complementary and Alternative Medicine,
http://nccam.nih.gov/health/meditation. Provides
information about meditation programs.

Obsessive Compulsive Anonymous, http://obsessivecompulsive
anonymous.org. Provides information about this group's
organization and shows where groups meet both in the
United States and internationally.

Obsessive-Compulsive Foundation, www.ocfoundation.org. A
great organization with excellent information and other
links.

Online Florida Obsessive-Compulsive Inventory OCD
Screening Test (FOCI), www.ocfoundation.org/
ocd-screening-test.html. Provided by the Obsessive-
Compulsive Foundation (original version created by
Wayne K. Goodman, M.D.).

Organized Chaos, www.ocfoundation.org/organizedchaos.
A Webzine from the OCF for teens and young adults
with OCD.

Partnership for Prescription Assistance (PPA), www.pparx.org.
This organization helps patients who cannot afford to pay
for medication receive services by connecting them to the
appropriate sources.

"The RIGHT Stuff—Obsessive Compulsive Personality
Disorder: A Defect of Philosophy, Not Anxiety,"
www.ocdonline.com/
articlephillipson6.php. An article by Steven Phillipson,
PhD, about OCPD.

Tourette Syndrome Association, www.tsa-usa.org. Provides
information on TS.

Trichotillomania Learning Center, www.trich.org. Gives helpful
information for people with TTM.

OCD RESIDENTIAL TREATMENT CENTERS

Here is a list of just a few of the residential treatment centers in the United States. If you type "OCD treatment centers" into a search engine, you may find one closer to your home. It is recommended that you also ask your mental health professional for a reputable center, as well as his or her opinion about whether this type of treatment will be helpful to you.

Menninger Clinic, Houston, Texas. A hospital treatment program for adolescents and adults who suffer from severe anxiety disorders, including OCD. For more on the OCD treatment program, visit www.menningerclinic.com or call (800) 351–9058 or (713) 275–5000.

The Obsessive-Compulsive Disorder Center at Rogers Memorial Hospital, Oconomowoc, Wisconsin. Offers treatment for both children and adults. For more information, go to www.rogershospital.org/hospital/ocd/ocd3.htm or call (800) 767–4411 or (262) 646–4411.

OCD Institute at the McLean Hospital, Belmont, Massachusetts. A treatment center for ages sixteen and older. Visit www.mclean.harvard.edu/patient/adult/ocd.php or call (617) 855–3279 for more information.

Appendix B: Mental Disorders Related to OCD

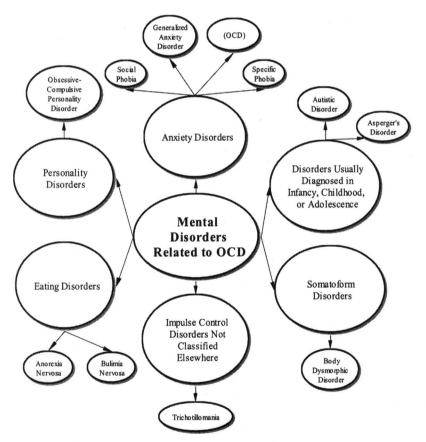

(classifications based on information from *Diagnostic and Statistical Manual of Mental Disorders: DSM-IV-TR*)

Glossary

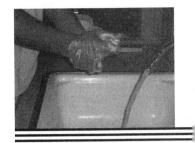

504 Plan: An individualized plan written by the parents, teachers, and school administrators of a student with special educational needs, outlining the student's needs and the accommodations that will be made; the name comes from Section 504 of the Rehabilitation Act of 1973, a legal document that allows students with disabilities, such as OCD, to receive proper education and accommodations.

acupuncture: An ancient Chinese treatment that uses needles for therapeutic purposes.

Americans with Disabilities Act (ADA): A law that ensures that individuals with disabilities receive equal opportunities in employment.

anorexia: An eating disorder that causes people to have a fear of becoming overweight.

anxiety: Distress caused by fear.

Asperger's Disorder (AD): A disorder that involves difficulty having relationships with others, odd and repetitive behaviors, and concentrated interest in limited areas.

attention-deficit/hyperactivity disorder (ADHD): A disorder that often involves hyperactivity, a short attention span, and lack of focus.

autism: A disorder that includes not using nonverbal behaviors (such as making eye contact), not wanting to share interests with others, having a delay in speech, and using repetitive behaviors.

basal ganglia: A part of the brain that controls motor function.

165

behavior therapy: A form of therapy that involves a therapeutic focus on altering one's behavior.

biofeedback: A type of therapy that uses machines to monitor one's bodily functions, such as heartbeat and blood pressure, with an aim toward teaching the patient to alter those functions.

biological: Related to the body, such as the brain.

body dysmorphic disorder (BDD): A disorder involving an unrealistic body image.

caudate nucleus: A part of the brain that selects and uses the appropriate action for a task.

cerebellum: A part of the brain involved with coordination and processing information.

cerebral cortex: The outer layer of the brain, the gray matter; it is split into lobes, each responsible for different functions.

cerebrum: The largest part of the brain, which is divided into two hemispheres, the left and right.

cognitive behavioral therapy (CBT): A form of therapy that involves changing one's actions and thoughts to lessen the occurrence of obsessions and/or compulsions.

comorbid: Two or more diseases or disorders that occur at the same time.

compulsion: An impulse to perform an action or behavior.

contamination: The state of having been exposed to something harmful or unclean.

coprolalia: The uncontrollable use of obscene language.

depression: A condition involving such symptoms as sleeplessness or oversleeping, extreme sadness, and hopelessness.

dopamine: A neurotransmitter in the brain that plays a part in motor function and reward.

Diagnostic and Statistical Manual of Mental Disorders (DSM): A manual that gives a list of the symptoms for mental disorders; it is used by mental health workers in diagnosis.

electroconvulsive therapy (ECT): A type of therapy that uses currents of electricity to shock the brain and help with neurotransmitter imbalances.

exposure with response prevention (ERP): A type of therapy in which the patient confronts his or her anxiety with the goal of reducing anxiety in the future.

frontal lobe: The part of the brain that controls motor activity and thinking.

General Educational Development (GED): Standardized tests given that, if passed, are equivalent to a high school diploma.

generalized anxiety disorder (GAD): A type of anxiety disorder characterized by excessive worry and physiological symptoms such as headaches and muscle tension.

genetics: A branch of biology that studies heredity.

habituation: To get "used to" something through exposure so that it becomes less frightening.

hereditary: Genetic characteristics that are passed from parents to children through genes.

hierarchy: A personal list of fears from least to most frightening.

hoarding: Accumulating a large number of items, often unnecessarily.

imaginal exposure: A script created using worst-case scenarios to provoke anxiety, with the intention of desensitizing the patient through repeated exposure.

impulse control disorder: A behavior that causes a person to feel the need to perform a certain action. Once performed, the person feels a release of tension and anxiety.

Individualized Education Plan (IEP): An individualized plan created for a student with a disability (by a teacher, parent, and school district representative) so that the student receives the proper modifications; it also lists goals for that student.

Individuals with Disabilities Education Act (IDEA): A federal act that ensures that students with disabilities receive the proper education.

magnetic resonance imaging (MRI): A machine that takes images of the body using magnets and radio waves.

meditation: A relaxation technique that uses both the mind and body.

mental illness: A disorder or disease of the mind.

neurotransmitters: Chemical substances, such as endorphins or dopamine, that nerve cells release in order to communicate with one another.

norepinephrine: A neurotransmitter and hormone.

obsession: An unreasonable preoccupation with a thought, feeling, or action.

obsessive-compulsive disorder (OCD): An anxiety disorder that includes such symptoms as repetitive thoughts or feelings and repetitive behaviors or actions to try to relieve the anxiety.

obsessive-compulsive personality disorder (OCPD): A personality disorder that includes such symptoms as perfectionism and lack of flexibility.

occipital lobe: The part of the brain that controls vision.

OCD spectrum disorder: A disorder similar to OCD that occurs along with OCD.

orbital cortex: The area of the brain that helps with controlling our actions; people with OCD are believed to have an overactive orbital cortex.

parietal lobe: The part of the brain responsible for the senses (except smell) and sensations, such as pain, temperature, and our understanding of the spatial organization of the world.

pediatric autoimmune neuropsychiatric disorders associated with streptococcal infections (PANDAS): A rare type of OCD that stems from a strep infection.

positron emission tomography (PET) scan: A technology that allows doctors to determine the activity of the brain.

psychiatrist: A medical specialist (who can prescribe medication) who works with individuals with mental illness.

psychoanalyst: A psychologist who concentrates on subconscious thoughts (thoughts the individual is unaware of).

psychologist: A type of therapist (who cannot prescribe medication) who works with individuals with mental illness.

ritualize: To make into a ritual or repetitive act.

schizophrenia: A psychotic disorder characterized by hallucinations, delusions, and a loss of reality.

scrupulosity: A form of OCD in which the person experiences the compulsion to pray to get rid of bad thoughts.

Section 504 of the Rehabilitation Act: See *504 Plan*.

selective serotonin reuptake inhibitor (SSRI): A type of medication that affects solely the neurotransmitter serotonin in the brain.

serotonin: A neurotransmitter responsible for processes such as depression as well as sleep and memory.

serotonin reuptake inhibitor (SRI): A type of medication that affects neurotransmitters in the brain, such as serotonin, norepinephine, and dopamine.

social phobia: An anxiety disorder in which a person has a fear of social situations.

specific phobia: An anxiety disorder in which a person has an intense fear of an object or situation.

temporal lobe: The part of the brain involved in hearing, speech, smell, taste, emotion, some memory, and some vision.

thalamus: A part of the brain that passes messages from the spinal cord to the cerebrum.

therapist: A mental health professional; this term can refer to a psychologist, psychiatrist, or psychoanalyst.

tic: A repetitive, uncontrollable movement; this can be a motor action or vocal sound.

Tourette syndrome (TS): A neurological disorder involving tics.

trichotillomania (TTM): An impulse disorder involving pulling hair from such places as the head, eyelashes, and eyebrows.

yoga: A form of exercise that concentrates on controlling the mind and body through proper breathing and body positions.

Index

Index

About the Author

Natalie Rompella has worked as an elementary and middle school teacher and has written and edited curricula for grades K through 8. She is the author of several books for children, including *Don't Squash That Bug!* and *Famous Firsts: The Trendsetters, Groundbreakers, and Risk-Takers Who Got America Moving!* She has dealt with having obsessive-compulsive disorder for the last nineteen years. To learn more about her, visit her Web site at http://natalierompella.com.